When **Grammar** Meets **Linguistics**

When Grammar Meets Linguistics

Jeong-Seok Kim

SEJIN

Preface

English grammar is very complex, and no one can be familiar with everything about it. However, it is possible for non-native speakers of English to master essential knowledge of English grammar. This book aspires to provide that knowledge. There has been a prolonged period of gestation of this book. It was first inspired by my lectures on English grammar at Yeungnam University in 2001. Although I moved onto Korea University in 2007, I could not stop thinking of writing an English grammar book from the perspective of linguistics.

This book is intended for high-intermediate and advanced students. I hope that more advanced students and instructors will also find it fruitful. It will highlight some of the abstruse points of English grammar that students have studied so far and present many more features of English grammar suitable for an advanced level of study. I offer students a body of terminology for a good and solid command of English grammar. Taking everything in is sometimes hard work, but it is ultimately rewarding.

The following combination of features makes this textbook a unique and practical resource for students. First, the keywords in the left or right margins are intended to assist students to grasp rules or explanations more esthetically and efficiently. Second, a modular approach to grammar breaks down a rather heterogeneous collection of topics from diverse origins into 20 manageable units. It is not necessary to go through the units in order. The units are organized so a student can go straight to a particular unit. Third, explanations and tips are written in clear and everyday language, so students will feel secure about rather than intimidated by grammar. The explanations above the examples are intended to be simple and straightforward. They take into account approaches to grammar developed by modern linguistic analysis, but employ the traditional grammatical terms as much as possible. Finally, the book includes consecutively numbered examples to facilitate communication between the instructor and students. The majority of these examples are authentic rather than made up. Many of them have been drawn from *The Washington Post* and the *Top 100* books chosen by BBC. Colloquial examples were often extracted from the words of characters in literary works.

To lend validity to this book, I consulted five ESL dictionaries: the *Cambridge Advanced Learner's Dictionary*, the *Collins Cobuild Advanced Learner's English Dictionary*, the *Longman Dictionary of Contemporary English*, the *Macmillan English Dictionary for Advanced Learners*, and the *Oxford Advanced Learner's Dictionary*.

I am indebted to Hikyoung Lee, Sang-Gu Kang, and Jee Young Lee, for the vision and direction they provided at every crucial stage in planning and writing of this book. I extend special thanks to my students for their substantial contributions to the final manuscript: Eun-Gyeong Bae, Da-eun Chang, MinYoung Cho, A Ram Jo, Duk-Ho Jung, Saw-Yeo Kang, Kihoon Kim, Kyung Mi Lee, Myung-Hee Nam, Ye Ji Oh, and Myung Hoon Park. Finally, I wish to thank my family for their unflagging support and patience.

I dedicate this book to my two daughters, Yijun and Yijae.

Jeong-Seok Kim
August 2012

Symbols and Conventions

A	Adjective
Adv	Adverb
AdvP	Adverb Phrase
AP	Adjective Phrase
Art	Article
Aux	Auxiliary
Conj	Conjunction
Det	Determiner
DO	Direct Object
ECM	Exceptional Case-Marking
GF	Grammatical Function
Gr	Grammar
IO	Indirect Object
MV	Main Verb
Neg	Negation
N	Noun
NP	Noun Phrase
NPI	Negative Polarity Item
Num	Number
P	Preposition
Part.	Participle
POS	Part of Speech
PP	Prepositional Phrase
PPI	Positive Polarity Item
PRO	Unpronounced Pronoun
ProN	Pronoun
PRED	Predicate
S	Sentence or Clause
SAI	Subject-Aux Inversion
sb	somebody
sth	something
SU	Subject
V	Verb
V-ingP	Verb Phrase starting with *-ing*
VP	Verb Phrase

*	ungrammatical
?	slightly degraded
??	more degraded than ?
#	semantic or pragmatic anomaly
' '	paraphrase
( )	The parenthetical expression is optional.
{A, B}	Choose either A or B, but not both simultaneously.
*( )	The parenthetical expression is mandatory.
(*)	With the parenthetical expression, the string is ungrammatical.

Co-numbering
Two NPs that have the same subscript index refer to the same entity.
(e.g.) $John_1$ criticized $himself_1$.
[*John = himself*]

+a, [$_{NP}$ Det (Num) ___ N]
A word whose POS is adjective appears in the underlined position which is followed by a noun and preceded by a determiner and an optional occurrence of number.

Contents

1 Sentence Sense

Sentence

A sentence is defined as follows:

(1) A sentence is a group of words, usually containing a verb, which expresses a thought in the form of a statement, question, instruction or exclamation and starts with a capital letter.

1.1 Types of Sentences: Complexity

Simple S

A simple sentence consists of a subject (e.g., noun phrase = NP) and a predicate (e.g., verb phrase = VP). In (2a) the subject is a single-membered NP. In (2b) the subject is a two-membered NP. In (3a) and (3b) the subject is a pronoun (ProN), which is a type of nouns (Ns). In this light, a ProN is regarded as a single-membered NP. In short, the subject in English is usually realized as an NP.

(2) a. Tickets are available free of charge from the department.

b. The bridge collapsed in the storm.

(3) a. I had new clothes and a new hairstyle.

b. She lives on campus.

Compound S

A compound sentence has two or more main clauses. Coordinators (= coordinating conjunctions) such as *and, but,* or *or* are used in the compound sentence.

(4) a. I cooked lunch, and I baked a cake.

b. I am sorry, but I cannot stay any longer.

c. Turn the heat down, or you will be burned.

Complex S

A complex sentence has one independent clause and at least one subordinate clause.

(5) a. I heard the rumor [that Danny kissed Tracie].

b. I haven't seen him [since I moved to Paris].

c. [Whether you stay home or not], I will go to the party.

Compound-Complex S

A compound-complex sentence consists of at least two independent clauses and at least one subordinate clause.

(6) I totaled my car, so I had to buy a new one, [though I had planned to wait].

1.2 Grammatical Function

POS

Each linguistic expression has a distinctive part of speech (POS): Verb (V), Preposition (P), Noun (N), Adjective (A), Adverb (Adv), Determiner (Det), Negation (Neg), Verb Phrase (VP), Prepositional Phrase (PP), Noun Phrase (NP), Adjective Phrase (AP), Adverb Phrase (AdvP), etc.

GF

Notions such as *subject*, *complement*, *object*, and *adjunct* (or *adverbial*) are not the names of POSs. They denote the grammatical function (GF) which a particular POS fulfills in a string or a sentence.

An element which appears in GF positions can be interpreted as a subject or an object regardless of its meaning. For example, in (7) the fact that people eat breakfasts and that breakfasts do not usually eat people is irrelevant insofar as the interpretation of these sentences is concerned. What is at stake is which position each argument occupies and which GF each argument has. This determines how to interpret the sentences.

(7) a. Lily ate her breakfast.
b. #Her breakfast ate Lily.♣

GF can be performed with clauses.

(8) a. **That he was tired** surprised us. [GF: Subject]
b. I understand **that animals get old and sick**. [GF: Object]

♣ As a convention, the prefixed pound sign (#) indicates semantic or pragmatic anomaly.

NP: Subject, Object, Complement

An NP plays the role of the subject or the object of a V.

(9) a. **Two children** were rescued.

b. **I** will tackle **the repairs**.

An NP functions as the complement of a linking V.

(10) a. It has become **an essential part of people's pastimes**.

b. It seemed **a good idea**.

An NP acts as the object of a P.

(11) a. The important information is at **the bottom of the page**.

b. He raised his hands above **his head**.

The (simple or core) subject agrees with its V. In (12c) the unit of [A and B] always agrees with a plural V.

(12) a. A dust **cloud** follows the galloping zebras.

b. His **critics** are all agents or accomplices of the West.

c. **Spring and fall** are my favorite seasons.

Adverbial/Adjunct

An adverbial (= adjunct) is instantiated as an AdvP, an NP, or a PP. We assume that in (13a) *clearly* is a single-membered AdvP.

(13) a. After he hit my head, I could not see [$_{\text{AdvP}}$ **clearly**].

b. The old man snored [$_{\text{NP}}$ **all night**].

c. Ross gave Rachel a gift [$_{\text{PP}}$ **in the evening**].

1.3 Types of Verbs

Regular Vs have four forms: base form, third person singular form, V-*ing* form, and V-*ed* form.

Regular V

(14)	a.	attack	attacks	attacking	attacked
	b.	marry	marries	marrying	married

The following shows types of irregular Vs. *Be* has the most irregular V forms in English.

Irregular V

(15)	let	lets	letting			[3 forms]
(16)	sell	sells	selling	sold		[4 forms]
(17)	eat	eats	eating	ate	eaten	[5 forms]
(18)	be	am/is/are	being	was/were	been	[8 forms]

Transitive Vs select one or two complements: monotransitive Vs as in (19a) and ditransitive Vs as in (19b) and (20a). The contrast in (20) indicates that *put* is ditransitive.

Transitive V

(19) a. The two parties have forged an alliance.

b. Robin bought her dad some flowers.

(20) a. She put the letter on the table.

b. cf. *She put the letter.♣

c. cf. *She put on the table.

♣ The star (*) indicates that the following string is not grammatical.

Intransitive V

Intransitive Vs optionally select adverbials.

(21) He sneezed (loudly).

Linking V

The following is called *linking* Vs. They link a subject with a subject complement.

(22) appear, be, become, feel, seem, smell, taste

(23) [The final scene] feels [like a moment on the verge of something else, rather than a tidy ending].

A complement is instantiated as an NP, an AP, or a PP.

(24) a. Ross is [$_{NP}$ a university professor].

b. Rachel was [$_{AP}$ (extremely) tired].♣

c. Joey is [$_{PP}$ in jail].

V-Group

A number of Vs can appear in a clause.

(25) a. They have proved him wrong.

b. You will meet some new friends at class.

c. She might have been a good doctor.

d. Barney would have been impressed by the athlete.

♣ The parenthesis notation ( ) indicates that the inside material is optional.

1.4 Types of Sentences: Force

Sentences are usually realized as declarative ones.

Declarative S

(26) From this production, one could surmise that Strassberger is a better set designer than a director.

In negative clauses, *not* appears after the first auxiliary (Aux) V.

Negative S

(27) a. I have **not** been there.
b. The whole face of the Earth would **not** have been changed.
c. The book must **not** have been being written.

Not is contracted as *n't*.

(28) a. I ca**n't** understand it!
b. Danny should**n't** leave.

English has two types of questions (= interrogative sentences). The following shows *yes/no* questions.

Interrogative S

(29) a. Did he feel all the better for the drink?
b. Have you lost ten kilos in weight?

The following shows wh-questions. Notice that there is no Subject-Aux Inversion (SAI) in the case of wh-subject questions.

(30) a. Who saw Mary? [wh-subject question]
b. What did you see? [wh-object question]
c. When did you see Mary? [wh-adverbial question]

The following shows a case of multiple wh-questions.

(31) Who saw what when where?

Exclamative S

A wide variety of constructions may be used for exclamations. As illustrated in (32), declarative sentences, interrogative sentences, free relatives, isolated NPs, inversion, and subordination to factive Vs such as *believe* are used for exclamations in English.

(32) a. He was so hungry!
 b. Isn't this great!
 c. How hungry we were!
 d. The speed they drive on the freeway!
 e. God, was I hungry!
 f. I can't believe how much he has grown!

Imperative S

In imperatives, bare Vs are used.

(33) a. **Do** your homework!
 b. **Be** nice!
 c. [In the elevator] Somebody **hit** five, please.♣
 d. Taylor Wilson is the youngest person to build a nuclear fusion reactor. For more information **tune** in to CNN Sunday at 2 p.m. ET.

♣ [ ] indicates a situation.

Imperatives with overt subjects may optionally have the ProN *you*, or indefinite ProN like *anyone* and *someone* in the subject position.

(34) a. You behave yourself!

b. Someone please go find a doctor.

Negative imperatives start with *do not*, *don't,* or *never*.

(35) a. Do not spread the word.

b. Don't behave like an infatuated teenager.

c. Never mind—you are all right now.

Imperatives are used to ask somebody to do something.

(36) Fetch me a drink of water.

Imperatives are used to give somebody advice or a warning.

(37) Watch your step!

Do imperatives sound more polite or more emphatic.

(38) a. Do be nice to yourself.

b. Do stop moving.

Written instructions may be uttered as imperatives.

(39) a. Shake well before being served.

b. [There is a sign near a newly painted area.] Don't touch!

Function words are often optional in imperatives.

(40) a. Find (a) pencil and (a) paper.

b. Erase (the) code number.

The pattern of [*let's* V] is used for a suggestion.

(41) Let's move on.

The pattern of [*do let's*] sounds more emphatic.

(42) **Do let's** start the project immediately.

The negative form of *let's* (= *let us*) is *let's not* or *don't let's*.

(43) a. **Let's not** make any trouble.

b. **Don't let's** make any trouble.

In the following, [*let* imperative] is not a suggestion but a mild obligation.

(44) If that is what he really intends to do, **let** him do so.
'..., he **should** do so.'♣

♣ Single quotations (' ') below an example indicate a paraphrased meaning of the example.

Tags of imperatives start with *will or would.*

(45) a. Hurry up, will you!

b. Open the door, would you?

Vocative imperatives start or stop with an addressee form, separated by a comma.

(46) a. Jenny, you go first.

b. Look what I found under the couch, dear.

In the following, the imperative clause is intended to be conditional, assuming a sort of hypothetical situation.

(47) Do it again, and I will kick you out!
'If you do it again, you will be kicked out by me.'

Exercise 1

1_1

Select the expression that best completes each sentence:

(48) A complex sentence contains one independent clause and at least one (dependent clause, adjective).

(49) A compound-complex sentence has at least two (independent, short) clauses and at least one dependent clause.

(50) In a compound-complex sentence, the dependent clause (cannot, can) be part of the independent clause.

1_2

Identify the part of the speech (POS) for the underlined word in each sentence:

[e.g.] The outside of the boat needs scraping. [Answer: Noun]

(51) You should scrape the boat without outside help.

(52) The ambulance is parked right outside the yard, next to the beehive.

(53) Turn right past the store with the neon sign in the window.

(54) Always follow through with what you start.

(55) The remark went right through one ear and out the other.

(56) The gardener mowed the lawn after he reread *Lady Chatterley's Lover*.

1_3

Underline every core (or simple) subject which agrees with the main verb in each sentence:

[e.g.] All of the displays feature artifacts still used by local tribes. The mammoth's shaggy coat and long tusks attract attention.

(57) A caption on one display provides a clue.

(58) What does that setting suggest?

(59) With lamp in hand each of them squeezes through the opening.

(60) In one room of the cavern black and red bulls dominate the walls.

(61) The city where my uncle lives is noisy.

1_4

Underline every noun (N), verb (V), adjective (A), and adverb (Adv) in each sentence, and then write its POS in parentheses:

[e.g.] The young (A) contestant (N) seemed (V) very (Adv) nervous (A).

(62) Some raucous members of the audience laughed too loudly at this silly comments.

(63) Its citizens were worldly and sophisticated.

1_5

Subordinate clauses perform a nominal (being subjects, objects, or complements), adjectival (modifying nominals), or adverbial (modifying non-nominals) function. Underline subordinate clauses in each sentence, and identify their grammatical function:

[e.g.] Even before the fire alarm sounded (adverbial function: modifies *sensed*), I sensed that something was happening (nominal function: direct object).

(64) I smelled smoke before I heard the fire alarm.

(65) The tragedy of life is that people don't change.

(66) The trouble with being in the rat race is that even if you win you're still a rat.

(67) Does every generation wonder how the former generation coped without modern inventions?

(68) Those who write clearly have readers; those who write obscurely have commentators.

1_6

Put the following words in the right order to make sentences:

[e.g.] Ring bells loudly the. [Answer: Ring the bells loudly.]

(69) Mary should stop smoking is clear that.

(70) Lions seven of the jungle ran out.

(71) She owns many cages bird antique beautiful.

2 Questions

When Grammar Meets Linguistics

2.1 *Yes/No* Questions

The following shows a *yes/no*-question.

(1) A: Are you hungry?

B1: Yes, I am hungry.

B2: No, I'm not hungry.

Short Reply

Short replies are very common in spoken English.

(2) A: Do you study English?

B: Yes, I do.

(3) A: Do you wish to be unmarried?

B: No, I don't.

Politeness

Note, however, that a short reply such as *Yes, you did* sounds more polite than just *Yes*, or than repeating back all the expressions uttered in the question.

(4) A: Did I embarrass you at the party?
B: Yes, you DID embarrass me at the party. [showing anger]

Aux

If you have one Aux or two, you front the (first) Aux in order to make *yes/no* questions.

(5) **Is** she ___ working on it?

(6) a. **Could** they ___ **have** done it?
b. ***Have** they **could** ___ done it?

do-support

If there is a main V, the dummy *do* is inserted in *yes/no* questions.

(7) a. **Do** they study Spanish?
b. **Does** he study Spanish?
c. **Did** he study Spanish?

have

Have questions have a couple of forms. (8b) is less common.

(8) a. **Does** he **have** a job?
b. **Has** he a job?

Negative *yes/no* questions are usually used to confirm an assumption.

(9) Didn't she complete her job?
'I was sure that she completed her job.'

2.2 Wh-Questions

Wh-questions have at least one wh-word.

(10) who whose whom which what
when where why how

The following shows wh-questions.

(11) Who has done the dishes?

(12) a. **With whom** were you talking? [pied-piping]♣

b. cf. **Whom** were you talking **with**? [P-stranding]

c. cf. **Who** were you talking **with**? [P-stranding]

d. cf. ?**With who** were you talking? [pied-piping]♣♣

Wh-adverbials trigger the Subject-Aux Inversion: *when, where, why,* or *how*.

(13) a. **When has** Mary done the dishes?

b. ***When** Mary **has** done the dishes?

♣ The Pied Piper of Hamelin (German: Rattenfänger von Hameln) is the subject of a legend concerning the departure or death of a great many children from the town of Hamelin (Hameln), Lower Saxony, Germany, in the Middle Ages. The earliest references describe a piper, dressed in pied (multicolored) clothing, leading the children away from the town never to return. In the 16th century the story was expanded into a full narrative, in which the piper is a rat-catcher hired by the town to lure rats away with his magic pipe. When the citizenry refuses to pay for this service, he retaliates by turning his magic on their children, leading them away as he had the rats. This version of the story spreads as a fairy tale. This version has also appeared in the writings of, among others, Johann Wolfgang von Goethe, the Brothers Grimm and Robert Browning. [Wikipedia]

♣♣ The question mark (?) before a string indicates that the following string is slightly degraded.

Who, whom, or *whose* refers to a person.

(14) a. Who saw Mary?

b. Whom did you meet yesterday?

c. Whose fault is it?

Which refers to a person or a thing.

(15) a. Which is your first daughter?

b. Which drink would you like?

2.3 Tag Questions

Statement, Tag

Tag questions consist of a statement (= stem) and a question tag. They are similar to *yes/no* questions. They ask somebody to agree or disagree. They sound more polite than *yes/no* questions. They are rarely used in formal written English.

(16) Barney is a nice guy, isn't he?

STATEMENT TAG

Intonation

The rising intonation on the question tag indicates that the speaker asks for information.

(17) Barney is a nice guy, isn't he?

The falling intonation on the tag indicates that the speaker expects the listener to agree with the information in the statement.

(18) Barney is a nice guy, isn't he?

The form of question tags is as follows: {Aux, main *be*} + ProN.♣

(19) a. I should apologize to her, shouldn't I?

b. Monica cooked meat very often, didn't she?

c. The sand martin is a brown bird, isn't it?

Have in tag questions has two forms. (20b) is less common.

have

(20) a. They have a beautiful home, don't they?

b. They have a beautiful home, haven't they?

In tag questions, a positive statement selects a negative question tag (*-n't*).

(21) Anything could happen in the next half hour, couldn't it?

The negative question tag with *I* is *aren't* instead of *amn't*, probably because the latter is hard to pronounce.

(22) a. I'm stylish, aren't I?

b. *I'm stylish, amn't I?

♣ To indicate mutually exclusive choices of elements in a string, we use the convention of curly brackets. For example, {α, β} = α or β. This convention states that if you choose α, you cannot choose β, but you should choose at least one; i.e., either α or β, but not both.

When a negative statement selects a positive question tag, you ask for help or information.

(23) He didn't criticize the school for trying to subdue individual expression, did he?

When a positive statement selects a positive question tag, you show reactions.

(24) a. Joey was subpoenaed to testify before the judge, was he? [surprise]

b. The campaign succeeded in raising public awareness, did it? [interest]

Politeness

An imperative with a question tag sounds more polite.

(25) a. Be succinct, will you?

b. Vote for the motion, won't you?

c. Pass me the pepper, would you?

When a negative imperative selects a question tag, the latter **must** be *will you*.

(26) Don't bet heavily on the races, will you?

Question tags may be used to emphasize impatience or anger.

(27) a. Oh, be patient, will you! [impatience]

b. Beware of falling asleep while studying, can't you! [anger]

The *let* imperative selects *shall we* as the question tag.

let

(28) Let's do the town, shall we?

I will selects *shall I*.

(29) I'll let the story out, shall I?

In modern English, the singular indefinite personal ProN subject in tag questions may select *they* in tags.

Descriptive Gr

(30) a. Everybody has their own ideas, don't they?

b. cf. *Everybody have their own ideas, don't they?

c. cf. All people have their own ideas, don't they?

(31) Nobody has seen my glasses, have they?

However, singular indefinite impersonal ProN subjects select *it* in tags.

(32) a. Everything in the capital is now quiet, isn't it?

b. Something has made you so mad, hasn't it?

There expletive statements select *there* in tags. This constitutes evidence that *there* is a subject in expletive constructions.

there

(33) There is a green hill far away, isn't {there, *it}?

When you answer a tag question, you should reply to the statement, not to the question tag. In the following, (34B) confirms a positive statement.

(34) A: The board suspended the program, didn't it?
B: Yes, it did.

In the following, (35B) negates a positive statement.

(35) A: The government has tried to offset the deficit, hasn't it?
B: No, it hasn't.

In the following, (36B) confirms a negative statement.

(36) A: The professor didn't notify his students of his schedule, did he?
B: No, he didn't.

In the following, (37B) repudiates a negative statement.

(37) A: Mickey doesn't know the answer, does he?
B: Yes, he does.

2.4 Indirect Questions

Ordering

Indirect questions retain the word order of declarative statements.

(38) I wonder if you could help me.

The following sounds more polite than (38) when you ask somebody to do something. What is the difference?

Politeness

(39) I was wondering if you could help me.

cf. Can you help me?

Normally, indirect questions do not require the Aux *do*. The Aux *do* is used only for emphasis. In the following, the capitalized word indicates that it receives phonetic prominence.

Emphasis

(40) I wonder what you {*did eat, DID eat} last night.

Indirect questions may be introduced with *if* or *whether*.

if, whether

(41) I wonder {if, whether} Costa Rica's Arenal volcano will erupt again.

Whether is especially preferred when there is a choice.

(42) I am wondering whether to have the pork or the fish.

The string *or not* **must not** immediately follow *if*.

(43) a. It depends on {whether or not, *if or not} she got the time.

b. It depends on {whether, if} she got the time or not.

2.5 Short Questions

A short question can be used as a short response.

(44) A: The barriers blunted the effect of the storm.

B: Oh, did they?

When a wh-question is used as a short response, the speaker asks for more information.

(45) A: Robin moved to Japan.

B: When?

(46) A: Finally, Ross got an A+.

B: Which class?

2.6 Other Questions

Alternative Q

Alternative questions provide two or more alternative answers.

(47) Would you like something to drink, coffee or tea?

Echo Q

Echo questions repeat all or part of what has been said.

(48) A: I saw Stacie yesterday.

B1: You saw who?

B2: You saw who yesterday?

Exclamatory questions can be used as exclamations, expressing the speaker's intention.

Exclamatory Q

(49) Gosh! Isn't that quick?

'It is really quick.'

Rhetorical questions need not be answered. They simply express the speaker's opinion.

Rhetorical Q

(50) A: I heard that you might move to London next year.

B: Who knows where I'll be next year?

Display questions take the shape of echo questions, and are often used by instructors to request that students display their knowledge about something.

Display Q

(51) So, last time, we discussed what?

Exercise 2

2_1

Complete these questions with the appropriate question tags:

(52) There are fascinating detours into the histories of science and mathematics, _____ ?

(53) You could write it for me, _____ ?

(54) Those proportions were higher in big cities, _____ ?

(55) The lawyer called the statement misleading, _____ ?

2_2

Put the words in parentheses in the right order to make sentences:

(56) He was wondering (worth, had, whether, been, it) the struggle.

(57) If you are writing about the visual design of an everyday object, (are, what, purposes, for, the, which) you use it?

(58) But honestly, where are they now and (they, lately, done, what, have)?

(59) He is also a brilliant orator, who knows (broad, his, charm, cheeky, how, smile, to, with) and outrageous sense of humor.

3 Negation

3.1 Verbal Negation

There is a negative word like *not* in negative sentences. *Not* can be contracted as *n't* in spoken and informal written English. *not*

(1) You {should **not**, should**n't**} say that.

The following shows contracted negations. Contraction

(2) a. isn't, aren't, wasn't, weren't
b. haven't, hasn't, hadn't
c. don't, doesn't, didn't
d. can't, couldn't
e. shouldn't, won't, wouldn't
f. daren't, needn't
g. mustn't, shan't, mightn't, oughtn't

You cannot contract *not* with an already shortened V. Why? (3b) and (4b) are hard to pronounce.

(3) a. It's not awful.
b. *It'sn't awful.

(4) a. They've not enough money.
b. *They'ven't enough money.

Note the following contrast. It is hard to pronounce *mn't* and *amn't*.

(5) a. I'm not stupid.
b. *I'mn't stupid.

(6) I'm a genius, {aren't, *amn't} I?

Ordering

Not is placed after the first V in a V group with two or more Vs.

(7) a. I had not ordered the chocolate cake for dessert.
b. They were not dressed for work.

In negative sentences, *be* behaves like an Aux.

(8) Marshall is not part of a consortium.

There are two options to negate *have*. *Have not* is less common.

(9) He {doesn't have, hasn't} wealth and power.

In order to negate V-*ing* or *to* infinitive, *not* is placed in front of it, respectively: +neg, [___ {V-ingP, *to* VP}].

(10) a. Ted is waving to Robin, not recognizing an old friend in a crowd.

b. He attempted not to pass the line.

Negative Q

Contracted negations must be used in negative questions.

(11) a. Shouldn't I visit my grandmother?

b. *Should not I visit my grandmother?

(12) a. Haven't you read the text?

b. *Have not you read the text?

(13) a. Isn't this bag yours?

b. *Is not this bag yours?

Negative questions can be interpreted as exclamations.

(14) Isn't this something!

Negative questions can be used in order to ask for an agreement.

(15) A: Isn't he Micky Stone?

B: Yes, he is.

If you are Korean (or Japanese), be careful when you answer negative questions.

(16) Aren't you afraid of a tiger?

a. Yes. 'I am afraid of a tiger.'

b. No. 'I am not afraid of a tiger.'

never

Never is placed after the first word in a V group.

(17) I **will never see** you again.

Never is placed before main Vs (MVs) and after the copular *be*: +adv, [{ ___ MV, *be* ___ }]

(18) a. I **never go** to the opera.

b. She **is never** disappointed.

Never precedes bare Vs in imperatives.

(19) **Never lie** to me.

neither ... nor

The only negative words allowed in one clause are *neither* ... *nor*.

(20) She has **neither** friends **nor** relatives to help her.

NPI

Negative polarity items (NPIs) like *any*, *anyone*, *anything*, and *yet* **almost always** appear in negative statements.

(21) a. My friend asked me for some money, but I did**n't** have **any**.

b. The mail has**n't** arrived **yet**.

Positive polarity items (PPIs) like *some*, *someone*, and *still* **normally** appear in positive statements.

PPI

(22) a. My friend asked me for **some** money, but I didn't have any.

b. Monica was **still** asleep when her husband went to work.

In negative raising as in (23), *not* moves from an embedded clause into a higher clause, and is combined with *do*. (23b) is preferred to (23a).

Negative Raising

(23) a. I think that dinner's **not** ready yet.

b. I do**n't** think that dinner's ready yet.

In verbal negation, PPIs change into the corresponding NPIs. The verbal negation *not* and the NPI *any* can be changed into a nonverbal negation like *no*.

(24) a. There is **something** wrong with him.

b. There is**n't** **anything** wrong with him.
'There is **nothing** wrong with him.'

(25) a. There is **some** wine in the bottle.

b. There is**n't** **any** wine in the bottle.
'There is **no** wine in the bottle.'

3.2 Nonverbal Negation

Not may appear in front of quantifiers as in (26a), frequency Advs as in (26b), or As as in (26c) in the form of nonverbal negation.

(26) a. Not all of the countries have proper hygiene regulations.

b. The rich are not always happy.

c. It is not unusual for women to watch the same movie several times.

No may precede an N in nonverbal negation.

(27) I have no time to lose.

Double Negation

Double negations are not allowed in standard English.

(28) You haven't seen {*nothing, anything} yet.

However, double negation involving *not* plus a negative prefix/word commonly appears in formal writing as in (29). It also occurs in the form of two negative elements in a phrase or a clause as in (30).

(29) Minimalism is a not uninterlesting linguistic theory.
'Minimalism is an interesting linguistic theory.'

(30) Professor Lee watched his approach not without enthusiasm.
'Professor Lee watched his approach with enthusiasm.'

None (of) is a negative indefinite ProN.

(31) a. They wanted some chips, but there was **none** left.

b. **None of** the children had enough to eat.

Nobody, nothing, no one (= no-one) and *nowhere* are negative words.

(32) a. The house was empty; **nobody** was there.

b. There is **nothing** in the paper.

c. **No one** could've hustled what you hustled today.

d. They were **nowhere** to be found.

Negative Prefix

Negative prefixes are attached to As, Advs, Ns, and Vs to negate the latter. The most common negative prefixes are *un-*, *in-*, *im-*, *il-*, *ir-*, *dis-*, *a-*, and *non-*.

(33)

	A	Adv	N	V
a.	**un**grateful	**un**gratefully	**un**gratefulness	
b.	**in**decent	**in**decently	**in**decency	
c.	**im**possible	**im**possibly	**im**possibility	
d.	**il**literate		**il**literacy	
e.	**ir**relevant	**ir**relevantly	**ir**relevancy	
f.	**dis**dainful	**dis**dainfully	**dis**dain	**dis**dain
g.	**a**symmetric	**a**symmetrically	**a**symmetry	
h.	**non**-specific	**non**-specifically	**non**-specification	**non**-specify

Exercise 3

3_1

Make these sentences negative:

(34) The vehicle appeared to have some damage from the incident.

(35) Operators might have adequate time for bathroom breaks.

(36) Either Mr. Bulaga or Mr. Malloy is keen for the general public to use his vehicles.

(37) There is something you can do.

3_2

Put the negative word in parentheses in the right place to make sentences:

(38) The guerrillas have enjoyed much public support. (never)

(39) Haddock and cod lie under the furthest rim of the ice, if they have not frozen to death too, but I have the strength the nerve to go out there, lacking a boat. (neither, nor)

(40) Thomas Anderson (Keanu Reeves), a software programmer in a world very much like our own who goes by his nighttime hacker moniker of Neo, has heard the Matrix whispered about his whole life, but one knows what it is. (no)

(41) That is allowed in Europe, but yet in America, where any such investment must be filed with the Securities and Exchange Commission. (not)

4 Nouns and Pronouns

4.1 Nouns

Countable N

Countable Ns are either singular or plural.

(1) a. a bank vs. banks
    b. the game vs. some games

Regular Plural N

Most of regular plurals take *-s*.

(2) puzzle puzzles

The Ns ending in *-o* take either *-s* or *-es*.

(3) a. photo photos
    b. potato potatoes

The Ns ending in a [vowel plus *-y*] take *-s*.

(4) essay essays

The Ns ending in a [consonant plus *-y*] take *-ies*.

(5) city cities

The Ns ending in *-ss*, *-ch*, *-s*, *-sh*, or *-x* take *-es*.

(6) a. class classes
b. inch inches
c. gas gases
d. wish wishes
e. box boxes

Irregular Plural N

The following shows irregular plurals.

(7) a. child children
b. foot feet
c. man men
d. mouse mice
e. tooth teeth
f. woman women

Det

Singular countable Ns should accompany a determiner (Det).

(8) a. An orange has lots of vitamin C.
b. We ordered another hamburger.
c. The dog growled again.

Plural countable Ns should not have an overt Det when they refer to people or things in general. In this generic usage, we may assume that a null (∅) Det exists. Null Det

(9) a. ∅ Dogs are faithful animals.
b. ∅ Players complained about distracting ringtones.

Some plural Ns are regarded as single items that have two linked parts. Linked N

(10) a. The trousers are pressed and ready to be worn.
b. He kept laughing the whole time I was taking down my suitcase and getting the scissors out for him.

Collective Ns refer to a group as a unit or as separate individuals. Collective N

(11) a. The majority is very large.
b. The majority of them are against the regulation.

Uncountable Ns cannot have plural forms. Uncountable N

(12) a. camping, photography, tennis
b. anger(*s), evidence(*s), ignorance(*s)

Some uncountable Ns in English have plural forms in other languages. In Korean, for instance, *money* and *furniture* are countable.

(13) Her investments make more money every year.

(14) a. The apartment is filled with antique furniture.
b. *We bought two furnitures.

Some uncountable Ns end in *-s*.

(15) a. Economics is often thought of as a science.

b. The news of a cure is encouraging.

Uncountable Ns cannot appear with *a*.

(16) Most retailers deliver (*a) new furniture to customers' homes and even truck away the old.♣

When uncountable Ns refer to specific things, they can appear with *the*.

(17) I helped Susan choose the furniture for her house.

Uncountable Ns cannot be modified by numbers. But they may be modified by *some*.

(18) I need {*two advices, some advice} about my car.

Sometimes, some uncountable Ns can be treated as countable Ns.

(19) a. Do you like coffee? [uncountable]

b. We asked for two coffees. [countable]

c. We asked for two cups of coffee. [uncountable]

♣ The star inside a parenthesis (*) indicates that the string is ungrammatical with the parenthetical expression.

Partitive

Partitives may select uncountable Ns.

(20) a. a bar of chocolate
b. two bits of advice
c. some items of furniture
d. three pieces of evidence cf. *three evidences
e. a stroke of luck

Some Ns can be either countable or uncountable. The indefinite article (Art) is used when something is a single unit. Otherwise, it is not used.

(21) a. Ross has started a new research.
b. Ross was doing research on ellipsis.

4.2 Pronouns

Anaphora

Anaphora refers to an anaphoric phenomenon (i.e., connection) between a ProN and its antecedent.

In forward anaphora, the antecedent precedes a ProN.

(22) Mike is smart. He could defend himself.

In backward anaphora (= cataphora), a ProN precedes the antecedent.

(23) When he took a roll, Professor Kim recognized that Rene was absent.

In intersentential (= across sentences) anaphora, a ProN and its antecedent are in separate sentences.

(24) Ross: Monica$_1$ asked Chandler$_2$ to put the plates$_3$ in the cupboard.♣
Rachel: To annoy her$_1$, he$_2$ stuffed them$_3$ in the closet.

ProN = Pro-NP

ProNs refer back to somebody or something. In fact, ProNs replace NPs. They are pro-NPs. That is, pronouns are misnomers. For the sake of convenience, however, we will use the term *pronoun* in this book.

(25) a. Phoebe wrote the lyric of the song.
b. His girlfriend wrote the lyric of the song.
c. That skinny hippie wrote the lyric of the song.
d. The odd skinny hippie wrote the lyric of the song.

(26) a. She wrote the lyric of the song.
b. *His she wrote the lyric of the song.
c. *That skinny she wrote the lyric of the song.
d. *The odd skinny she wrote the lyric of the song.

4.2.1 Personal Pronouns

Subject ProN

The following is the list of subject personal ProNs.

(27)

I	we
you	you
he, she, it	they

♣ Two NPs that have the same subscript index refer to the same entity.
(e.g.) John$_1$ criticized himself$_1$. [*John = himself*]

The following is the list of object personal ProNs.

Object ProN

(28) me us
you you
him, her, it them

According to Prescriptive Grammar, subject ProNs should appear in the subject complement position. However, object ProNs are frequently allowed in modern English.

Descriptive Gr

(29) A: Who is it?
B1: It's I.
B2: It's me. [prescriptively ill-formed, but descriptively well-formed]

Similarly, contrary to prescriptive rules, object ProNs are used in reduced comparative clauses.

(30) a. Ted is taller than I.
b. Ted is taller than me. [prescriptively ill-formed, but descriptively well-formed]

Ps can take a ProN as their complement.

(31) I got the truth from talking with her.

You and *they* can talk about people in general. They are generic ProNs.

Generic ProN

(32) a. If you are bored, you feel tired and impatient.
b. They say some of the best effects in my garden have been the result of serendipity.

In formal English, *one* refers to people in general.

(33) a. **One** can never be too careful.

b. Great books make **one** think.

4.2.2 Demonstratives

Demonstrative ProN

English has four demonstrative ProNs: *this, these, that*, and *those*. *This* and *these* refer to nearby people or things.

(34) a. You should read **this**.

b. I am taking **these** to my sick neighbor.

That and *those* refer to distant people or things.

(35) a. **That** needs help.

b. **Those** need help.

Anaphora

Demonstrative ProNs may refer back to things that were previously mentioned.

(36) a. It's driving me crazy, **this**.

b. There might be several problems in this approach. **These** will be discussed in the next chapter.

(37) a. It's a specialty, **that**.

b. Two boxes of photos have been delivered. **Those** are in the kitchen.

Demonstrative ProNs may refer forward to things that you will mention. Cataphora

(38) a. This is what I want, a big office with a fine view.

b. These are the topics we will be looking at next week: Prescriptive Grammar, Descriptive Grammar, Competence, Performance, and Universal Grammar.

Demonstrative ProNs behave like Dets in a pre-nominal position. In this case, they are called *demonstrative As*. Demonstrative A

(39) a. You should read this book.

b I am taking these flowers to my sick neighbor.

(40) a. That person needs help.

b. Those people need help.

When you simply do not want to repeat the same information as in (41a) or contrast two items of the same type as in (41b), you can use *one* or *ones*. Pro-*one*

(41) a. He looked for a pen and found one in his pocket.

b. The new kids are smarter than the old ones.

One refers to a nominal element which is bigger than an N but less than a full-fledged NP. In this sense, *one* is called a pro-N'.

(42) John wants [$_{NP}$ that big book of poems with the red cover], but Mary wants

a. *one.

b. this one.

c. this small one.

d. this small one with the blue cover.

e. *this small one of essays with the blue cover.

4.2.3 Reflexive Pronouns

Reflexive ProNs depend on an antecedent for their reference. They usually get their reference from the subject of a sentence.

(43)	myself	ourselves
	yourself	yourselves
	himself, herself, itself	themselves

Nonemphatic

Reflexive ProNs have two functions: emphatic and nonemphatic functions. In their nonemphatic function, reflexive ProNs appear with reflexive Vs. They are obligatory elements in a sentence.

(44) a. Joey poured *(himself) a glass of milk.

b. Make sure you behave *(yourself) when we visit the dean.

Emphatic

In their emphatic function, reflexive ProNs can appear in several different positions. They are optional elements in a sentence.

(45) a. It must be true that she's leaving because she told me so herself.

b. It must be true that she's leaving because she herself told me so.

c. It must be true that she's leaving because herself she told me so.

4.2.4 Reciprocal Pronouns

English has only two reciprocal ProNs: *each other* and *one another*. They indicate that an action is performed by two or more individuals.

(46) a. The puppies all chased each other.

b. They are highly suspicious of one another.

4.2.5 Indefinite Pronouns

The following shows indefinite ProNs.

(47) a. anybody, anyone, anything

b. everybody, everyone, everything

c. nobody, no one, nothing

d. somebody, someone, something

Indefinite ProNs are pronouns that do not refer to any people or things in particular.

(48) a. I have not told anyone.

b. Someone must have seen what happened.

c None of my children have blonde hair.

An indefinite ProN subject agrees with a singular V.

(49) a. Everyone {has, *have} their own ideas.

b. Everything in the kitchen {was, *were} destroyed by the fire.

Gender-free writing discourages writers from using the third person singular masculine ProNs with indefinite ProNs antecedents. (50a) was popular in the male-dominating society. (50b) is really gaining momentum along with the growing concern for feminism. (50c) seems to be still popular although the disjunction *or* sounds a bit awkward. The use of *his or her* sometimes sounds slightly formal, and it is becoming more common to use the plural ProN *their* as in (50d), which is allowed in modern English despite the agreement problem as discussed before. (50e) is the best option according to *Harbrace*.

(50) a. Everyone has his own way of dealing with problems.
b. Everyone has her own way of dealing with problems.
c. Everyone has his or her own way of dealing with problems.
d. Everyone has their own way of dealing with problems.
e. All the people have their own way of dealing with problems.

Indefinite personal ProNs may take an apostrophe *s* (’*s*).

(51) a. It is used primarily to authorize someone’s imprisonment without trial.
b. It’s nobody’s fault.

However, indefinite impersonal ProNs do not normally permit an apostrophe *s* (’*s*).

(52) a. *something’s cause
b. the cause of something

The pattern of [*some* α] indefinite ProNs is used in positive clauses.

(53) a. **Somebody** told me she lives near here.

b. I could hear **someone** crying in the next room.

The indefinite ProN [*some* α] may be used in interrogative sentences expecting a positive answer.

(54) Would you like **something** to drink?

The indefinite ProN [*any* α] may be used as the subject or object in declarative sentences.

(55) a. **Anyone** can go.

b. He couldn't see **anything**.

The indefinite ProN [*any* α] may be used in both positive and negative interrogative sentences.

(56) a. Has **anyone** seen my glasses **anywhere**?

b. Didn't you do **anything** wrong?

The indefinite ProN [*no* α] cannot be used with the negator *not*. (57b) and (58b) are ungrammatical due to the double negation.

(57) a. I have **nothing** new to tell you.

b. *I do**n't** have **nothing** new to tell you.

(58) a. **Nobody** agrees with me.

b. ***Nobody** does**n't** agree with me.

There are indefinite Advs such as {*anywhere, everywhere, nowhere, somewhere*}.

(59) a. He could meet Miss Marple **anywhere** in London.
b. I looked **everywhere** for my keys.
c. Flattery gets you **nowhere**.
d. You must have put your keys **somewhere**!

The pattern of {indefinite ProNs, Advs *else*} refers to people or things in addition to somebody or something already mentioned.

(60) a. You will have to wait for your turn like **everybody else**.
b. We can go **somewhere else** to talk.

4.2.6 Possessives

Possessive A

Possessives consist of possessive As and possessive ProNs. The following illustrates possessive As.

(61)

my	our
your	your
his, her, its	their

The word order in NPs dictates that possessives precede nominal or adjectival modifiers which precede the head noun: [$_{NP}$ possessive N/A N].

(62) a. Yijun is {my first daughter, *first my daughter}.
b. He left {his black leather jacket, *black leather his jacket} behind.

Possessive ProN

The following illustrates possessive ProNs.

(63) mine ours
yours yours
his, hers theirs

An N may take an apostrophe *s* ('*s*).

(64) a. I like the smartphone's functions.
b. It's nice to bring a smile to people's faces.

Plural Ns ending in -*s* just take an apostrophe (').

(65) I am going to visit [Richard's parents]' new house.

However, people's names ending in -*s* take an apostrophe *s* ('*s*).

(66) Can you explain Ross's island constraints?

Names conjoined by *and* may take an apostrophe *s* ('*s*) as in (67a). This usage suggests that an apostrophe *s* ('*s*) is a phrasal inflection. (67b) also shows that it is a phrasal inflection.

(67) a. Joey had to be rescued when [Monica and Chandler]'s apartment caught fire.
b. [the professor of psychology]'s lecture

The pattern of [a name or N + an apostrophe *s* ('*s*)] produces a missing phenomenon.

(68) a. She went to **Barney's**.

b. I am going to visit **Professor Kim's**.

Time expressions may have an apostrophe *s* ('*s*).

(69) a. **today's** news

b. **twenty minutes'** absence

c. **8 weeks'** recess

In addition to the apostrophe *s* ('*s*) possession, English has *of* possession.

(70) a. Some **of** my best friends showed up.

b. Students are supposed to read each chapter **of** the text.

In the following, *of* selects a possessive ProN or [N with '*s*].

(71) a. I share an office with a friend **of mine**.

b. A friend **of my second daughter's** drew that picture.

Own is an emphasizer for possessive expressions.

(72) a. Sarah, a blind Chihuahua, has **her own** seeing-eye companion.

b. Just two days after her wedding, Estrella Carrera, 25, was found stabbed to death in **her own** bathtub.

There are four types of preference regarding the choice of the apostrophe *s* possession and the *of* possession.

Preference

Animated NPs prefer the apostrophe *s* ('*s*) possession.

(73) a. Robin's sister

b. ?the sister of Robin

(74) a. the cat's fish

b. ?the fish of the cat

Inanimate NPs prefer the *of* possession.

(75) a. the legs of the chair

b. ??the chair's legs♣

Long NPs are usually expected to take the *of* possession.

(76) a. the dog of the people next door when I was a kid

b. ??the people next door when I was a kid's dog

A possessive Det cannot appear after *of* in the pattern of [*of* ProN].

(77) a. my destiny

b. *the destiny of my

c. the destiny of mine

♣ The double question mark (??) before a string indicates that the following string is more degraded than ?.

4.3 Pro-forms

Some predicates such as {*think, hope, expect, imagine, suppose, be afraid, guess*} select *so*. In the following, *so* refers to a clause. In this light, *so* can be called a Pro-S.

(78) A: I hope that Rachel feels better soon.
B: I hope so.

(79) A: I suppose she left late and got caught in traffic.
B: I suppose so.

(80) A: I expect him to arrive very soon.
B: I expect so.

As shown below, [V *so*] is negated as either [*not* V *so*] or [V *not*]. [V *not*] sounds more formal.

(81) A: I suppose that all the tickets have been sold now.
B: {I don't suppose so, I suppose not}.

(82) A: He ought to resign immediately.
B: {I don't think so, I think not}.

(83) {I don't imagine so, I imagine not}, considering statements like yours.

(84) As to a third season, {I didn't expect so, I expected not}.

However, you say *I hope not* and *I'm afraid not*, and *I guess not*.

(85) A: His cancer will be fatal.

B: {I hope not, *I don't hope so}.

(86) A: It's just simple as that.

B: {I'm afraid not, *I'm not afraid so}.

(87) A: Will Susan be at the cinema?

B: {I guess not, *I don't guess so}.

Exercise 4

4_1

Select the word that best completes each sentence, according to Prescriptive Grammar:

(88) The best dressed employee has always been (him, he).

(89) The winning contestants are the Bushes and (they, them).

(90) The concept that intrigued (we, us) had not yet been publicized.

(91) The thunderstorm frightened my cat and (I, me).

(92) Please sit next to Rachel and (me, I).

(93) (Kids', Kid's) play has moved to tablets and PCs.

4_2

Select the pronoun that best completes each sentence:

(94) I have two sisters. One is a doctor and (other, the other) is a nurse.

(95) I don't have to go there, (too, either).

(96) This is too small for me. Show me (another, other).

(97) Do you have any idea? Yes, I have a good (one, it).

(98) He bought me two shirts. But I like (either, neither) of them.

(99) To say is one thing and to do is (another, the other).

(100) The CEO of 3D Systems Corp demonstrates a home 3-D printer, which can print (something, anything) from shoes to prosthetics.

4_3

Select the correct form of the verb that agrees with the subject in each sentence:

(101) A combination of natural beauty, low off-season hotel rates, and interesting shops (makes, make) Park City, Utah, a wonderful summer destination.

(102) Donald Duck comics (was, were) banned from Finland because he doesn't wear pants.

(103) Seventy-five dollars (is, are) a lot to pay for one textbook.

(104) The evening news (continues, continue) to be filled with sad events.

(105) Economics (is, are) a required course for business majors.

(106) The university's board of trustees (is, are) divided on whether to raise student fees.

(107) The new board of our condominium association (plans, plan) to repave our parking lot.

(108) The team usually (agrees, agree) about where to go for dinner after practice.

(109) German measles (causes, cause) some birth defects.

(110) Neither of those restaurants (is, are) accessible to people in wheelchairs.

(111) All of the desserts (needs, need) to be refrigerated immediately.

(112) All of the furniture (is, are) on sale this week.

4_4

Find errors and correct them in the following sentences:

(113) These aren't my socks. These over there is my socks.

(114) I know those boys. He is my classmates.

(115) Look at this umbrella over here. They are mine.

(116) A: What do you want to buy?

B: I'd like to buy two slice of bread and some sugars.

(117) There have been many studies about the effect of television violences on children.

5 Determiners

Det

Determiners (Dets) are placed at the front of an NP.

(1) a. **all** his new articles

b. **that** handsome guy

c. **several** thousand people

d. **the** first fifty dates

Specific Det

Specific Dets such as the definite Art, demonstrative As, or possessive As refer to people or things that have already been mentioned.

(2) a. definite Art: the

b. demonstratives: this, that, these, those

c. possessives: my, your, his, her, its, our, their

(3) a. **The** man stopped me to ask what time it was.

b. I am taking **these** flowers to **my** sick neighbor.

General Det

General Dets refer to people or things for the first time or describe them in general.

(4) a. Barney has an idea for a good party.

b. We had much rain this summer.

The following general Dets select singular countable Ns.

(5) a, an, another, any, each, either, every, neither, no

(6) He loves another lady now.

The following general Dets select plural countable Ns.

(7) all, enough, many, no, some, any, few, more, other, both, fewer, most, several

(8) Albert had fewer ambitions ten years ago.

The following general Dets select uncountable Ns.

(9) all, any, enough, less, little, more, most, much, no, some

(10) Barney has enough money to pay the bills.

The following general Dets **cannot** select uncountable Ns.

(11) a, an, another, both, each, either, every, few, many, neither, several

(12) a. *each money

b. *several furniture

Most of the Dets play the role of ProNs. *The, a, an, every, no* and possessive As are exceptions.

(13) {All, *Every} enjoyed the movie.

The indefinite Art can be replaced with the numeral *one*.

(14) Ross has only one child.

5.1 Articles

Definite Art

Definite Arts may refer to particular people or things that you are familiar with.

(15) a. Has Lily locked the door?

b. Ted will meet Robin outside the main entrance.

c. The student asked his former professor what he should do.

d. "Afterward, the doctor asked me, 'How was that?' I reached up and gave him a big hug. These human gestures of forgiveness, caring, and compassion made a deep impression on me and on the kind of person I wanted to become."

The may refer to somebody or something that has been uttered in the previous discourse.

(16) Stacie brought me some bread and coffee, but the bread was stale and the coffee tasted of soap.

The is used to refer to a unique one in the world.

(17) a. Tonight and tomorrow night, look up at the sky for a spectacular light show.

b. The U.N. Security Council is expected to meet on Saturday.

The pattern of [*the* + singular countable N] may indicate a general statement about somebody or something.

(18) The smartphone has changed many people's lives in so many ways.

The pattern of [*the* + singular countable N] suggests system or service.

(19) a. I heard it on the radio.

b. Ross will put it in the mail for Rachel tomorrow.

The pattern of [*the* + name of a musical instrument] suggests somebody's ability to play the instrument.

(20) a. Yijun plays the piano.

b. Yijae is learning the flute.

Normally, *the* should not appear prior to proper Ns of people as in (21a). However, *the* may appear before proper Ns when they refer to a family as in (21b).

(21) a. *the Stone

b. Stacie has been living with the Stones for nearly six months.

The is used with nominals indicating some titles.

(22) a. the Queen of England
b. the Secretary-General of the United Nations
c. the President of South Korea

The is used with nominals indicating buildings.

(23) a. The Address Downtown Dubai is a skyscraper rising 306 meters.
b. The Great Mosque of Kairouan is located in the city of Kairouan, Tunisia.

The is used with nominals indicating newspapers.

(24) a. the LA Times
b. the Washington Post

The is used with nominals indicating a work of art.

(25) a. the Mona Lisa
b. the Angelus

The is used with nominals indicating a country.

(26) a. the United Kingdom
b. the United States of America

The is not used with nominals indicating countries that have singular Ns as their names.

(27) (*the) Korea

The is used with nominals indicating names of mountain ranges.

(28) a. the Alps

b. the Rocky Mountains = the Rockies

The is not used with nominals indicating names of individual mountains.

(29) a. (*the) Everest

b. (*the) Kumkang

The is used with nominals indicating names of a group of islands.

(30) a. the Bahamas

b. the Hawaiian islands

The is not used with nominals indicating names of individual islands.

(31) (*the) Pokonji Dol, a small Croatian island in the Adriatic Sea

The is used with nominals indicating areas of a country which contain *north*, *south*, *east*, or *west* as in (32a). There are some exceptions as in (32b). *The* is not used before the pattern of [{northern, southern, eastern, western} + a singular name] as in (32c).

(32) a the south of England, the north of England

b. South Europe, North Europe

c. southern Mexico, northern Mexico

The is used with nominals indicating names of areas of water (e.g., seas, oceans, rivers, canals, gulfs, straits).

(33) a. An offshore installation manager (OIM) at BP, Jonelle knows what it's like to be in charge of the health and safety of 80 workers on an oil platform in the North Sea.

b. Although the U.S. military has tens of thousands of troops stationed at long-standing bases in Japan, South Korea and Guam, as well as the island of Diego Garcia in the Indian Ocean, it is seeking to solidify its presence in Southeast Asia.

c. A man found dead Monday in the Potomac River has been identified as 23-year-old Muhammad H. Rehman of Alexandria, police said Tuesday.

d. In 1956, President Dwight Eisenhower condemned an Israeli-European attack on the Suez Canal.

e. Of course, only one country in recent days has threatened to close access to the Strait of Hormuz, the Persian Gulf bottleneck through which almost one-fifth of the world's oil supply flows.

The is not used with nominals indicating lakes.

(34) a. (*the) Lake Michigan

b. The More Safari for Less includes round-trip air from Washington Dulles to Nairobi; one night at the Ark Lodge in Aberdare National Park; two nights at Lake Naivasha, with an afternoon walk at the Crescent Island Wildlife Sanctuary and a full-day game drive to Lake Nakuru National Park.

The is not used with nominals indicating {continents, cities}.

(35) a. As multinational corporations from (*the) North America, Western Europe, Japan, and South Korea stormed into the emerging markets, many local companies lost market share or sold off businesses but some fought back.

b. His career was going well in (*the) New York, but would moving to China take him to the next level?

The pattern of [*the* A] denotes people in general. When [*the* A] is used as a subject, it agrees with a plural V.

(36) a. Phoebe devoted her life to helping the poor.

b. The poor are not always unhappy.

The pattern of [*the* + nationality A] denotes the people who come from a country. When [*the* + nationality A] is used as a subject, it agrees with a plural V.

(37) a. There were wars between the French and the English.

b. The Korean eat a lot of kimchi.

The is allowed to appear before a superlative form.

(38) Grifting is the sweet art of the con. But the sweetest con of all is to con another grifter.

Indefinite Art

Indefinite Arts are used before a singular countable N.

(39) Barney has an idea.

A is used when the following word begins with a consonant sound. *An* is used instead of *a* when the following word begins with a vowel sound.

(40) a. a group, a vowel, a liar

b. an office, an umbrella, an adult

Indefinite Arts are used when a single person or thing is mentioned for the first time.

(41) a. Joey needs **a dictionary**.

b. Marshall became **a lawyer**.

Indefinite Arts may select nominals indicating *whole numbers* as in (42a), *fractions* as in (42b), *money* as in (42c), *weights* as in (42d), or *measures* as in (42e).

(42) a. a hundred

b. a half

c. a dollar

d. a kilo

e. a yard

Null Art

It has been often argued that null Art exists before plural countable Ns as in (43a) or abstract Ns as in (43b), which is represented as ∅. Null Art does not have a sound, but it refers to people or things in general.

(43) a. **∅ Dogs** are faithful animals.

b. **∅ Flattery** gets you nowhere.

Generic Reference

Generic reference to a species or class can be made with a definite Art, an indefinite Art, or null Art.

(44) a. The tiger is a large fierce animal.

b. A tiger is a large fierce animal.

c. ∅ Tigers are large fierce animals.

5.2 Quantifiers

Quantifiers are a type of Dets indicating the quantity or number of something.

(45) all, any, both, every, each, (a) few, less, (a) little, many, most, much, several

All may select {plural countable Ns, uncountable Ns}.

(46) a. All students deserve a compliment.

b. Danny spent all his money.

Most may select {plural countable Ns, uncountable Ns}.

(47) {Most shops, *Most shop} will be closed tomorrow.

(48) Most research in this field has been carried out by UCONN linguists.

No may take {singular countable Ns, plural countable Ns, uncountable Ns}.

(49) a. Albert is **no friend** of his.

b. **No trains** will be affected by this weather.

c. There is **no butter** in the fridge.

Unlike *no*, *all, most,* and *none* can be used as ProNs.

(50) a. **All** of our equipment has been checked.

b. **Most** of us like watching movies.

c. {**None**, ***No**} of the foods are rotten.

According to *Cobuild*, when *none of* is followed by a plural countable N or ProN, the V is usually plural, but can be singular as in (51). This instruction is a bit dubious. (52) are from *Harbrace*. Can you make a generalization?

Prescriptive Gr

(51) a. None of **us are** the same.

b. None of **them has** lasted very long. [Correction: *has* → *have*]

(52) a. None of **those are** spoiled.

b. None of the **food is** spoiled.

All the takes {plural countable N, uncountable N}.

(53) a. A lexicon lists **all the words** found in the language.

b. A small change can make **all the difference** between a natural class and a non-natural class.

Quantifier Floating

Quantifier floating optionally moves the quantifier *all* rightward from a position in a subject NP to a position preceding the main V or after it. *All* is used for emphasis.

(54) a. All the students are coming.

b. The students all are coming.

c. The students are all coming.

Both refers to two people or things together, and takes plural Ns. *Either* refers to a choice between two people or things, and takes singular Ns. *Neither* refers to each of two people or things in the negative way, and takes singular Ns.

(55) a. Both birds sang loudly.

b. Ross had a book in either hand.

c. Neither student answered.

Both may take specific Dets.

(56) Both the students are invited.

Note the word order within the following NPs: [{*both of, either of, neither of*} + specific Det + plural Ns].

(57) a. Both of the students are invited.

b. Either of the students are invited.

c. Neither of the students are invited.

In the following, {*both of, either of, neither of*} take ProNs.

(58) a. Both of them are invited.

b. Either of them are invited.

c. Neither of them are invited.

The quantifiers *all*, *both*, and *each* may appear either before a ProN (with *of*) or after a ProN in the verbal object position.

(59) a. They invited all of them.

b. They invited them all.

(60) a. I liked both of them.

b. I liked them both.

(61) a. I want each of you to fill out the application form.

b. I want you each to fill out the application form.

According to *Cobuild*, *neither of* is normally used with a singular V, but it can be used with a plural V as in (62). However, consider the data in (63) provided by *Harbrace*. Can you make a generalization?

Prescriptive Gr

(62) a. Neither of us was having any luck. [Correction: *was* → *were*]

b. Neither of the children were there.

(63) a. Half or more of the population in west Texas is Hispanic.

b. Half or more of the people in west Texas are Hispanic.

Correlative Conj

The following shows correlative conjunctions, which join words, phrases, or clauses.

(64) a. Both professors and students have complained about the regulation.

b. Either you answer now or I leave!

c. Neither my first daughter nor my second daughter watched TV.

Quantifiers such as {*much, little*} are used with uncountable Ns. They show amount.

(65) a. I don't get much opportunity.

b. There is so little choice.

Much especially appears in negative sentences or negative questions.

(66) a. I don't make much money.

b. Don't you spend too much (money) on books?

Quantifiers such as {*so much, too much*} appear in positive sentences.

(67) a. Marshall spent so much time with Lily.

b. There is too much noise.

Quantifiers such as {*many, few*} are used with countable Ns. They show number.

(68) a. Sue doesn't have many DVDs.

b. Barney needs to get a few things.

Quantifiers such as {*a lot of, lots of, plenty of*} appear in positive sentences.

(69) a. Barney makes **a lot of money**.

b. Lily eats **lots of fruit**.

c. I've got **plenty of time**.

Usage

A few indicates a small number of people or things to mean *some*. *Few* is used with plural Ns to mean *not many*.

(70) a. I have **a few friends**.
'I have some friends.'

b. I have **few friends**.
'I do not have enough friends.'

Both *a few* and *few* are used with a plural verb.

(71) a. In software development, by contrast, **a few** big ideas **are** often more important than manufacturing precision, so the industry is often marked by a freewheeling culture—a culture that would be a little scary in the case of a medical equipment manufacturer.

b. Brazil's embassy in Washington is small; **few** of its firms **have** offices in the city.

Quantifiers such as {*few, little, very few, very little*} have negative connotations.

(72) a. I must say, though, that nobody would think you had any brains in your head to hear your usual line of talk. Actually, you've got a logical mind. **Few people** have.

b. There is **little time** to prepare for the mid-term exam.

c. Very few managers attend the meetings.

d. I've encountered very little danger in my life.

Quantifiers such as {*a few, a little*} have positive connotations.

(73) a. There were a few (students) who failed the course.

b. I have managed to save a little money.

The quantifier *more* takes {uncountable Ns, plural countable Ns}.

(74) a. Robin wants to spend more time with her dad.

b. No more excuses!

The quantifier *less* takes uncountable Ns.

(75) Students are likely to put less emphasis on being visionary.

The quantifier *some* is used with {uncountable Ns, plural countable Ns} to mean an amount of something or a number of people or things when the amount or number is not precise.

(76) a. Monica will make some coffee.

b. Rene brought me some flowers.

The quantifier *some* usually appears in positive statements.

(77) a. I could use some advice.

b. *I couldn't use some advice.

When the quantifier *some* appears in questions, a positive reply is expected.

(78) Would you like **something** to drink**?**

When the quantifier *some* appears with a singular N, it means *a certain*.

(79) **Some student** sent me an e-mail last night, but didn't identify himself or herself.

The quantifier *any* selects {plural Ns, uncountable Ns}. It refers to a number or an amount of something, usually in questions and negative statements.

(80) a. Are there **any cookies** left**?**

b. Phoebe has**n't** got **any money**.

The quantifier *any* may take singular countable Ns to refer to one of a number of people or things when it does not matter which person or thing is involved.

(81) a. **Any question** will be fine.
'The exact nature or identity of a question is not important.'

b. As **any teacher** can attest, the culture of a school—in large part determined by the leadership—has huge implications for the learning that happens there.

No means *not any*.

(82) Phoebe means **no harm**.
'Phoebe does**n't** mean **any harm**.'

The quantifier *another* means *an additional person or thing*.

(83) a. By ending selective prosecutions, pardoning imprisoned political leaders without conditions, and ensuring free and fair elections this fall, Yanukovych could become the leader who anchors Ukraine to Europe. If he fails to do so, he will be yet **another (politician)** to disappoint Ukrainians.

b. Mel and Rene got **another** ten day's journey.

The quantifier *other* takes plural countable Ns.

(84) a. Lasnik has **other articles** beside these.

b. The facile conclusion that our animal brains automatically fear people of **other races** is probably not right.

The quantifier *the other* takes {singular, plural} countable Ns.

(85) a. Shut **the other eye**.

b. Tracie likes this book, but I like **the other ones**.

Usage

Each and *every* have slightly different meanings. *Each* is used to refer to every one of two or more people or things when you are thinking about them separately, one by one.

(86) Each answer is worth 5 points.
'All answers are worth 5 points one after another.'

Every is used with singular Ns to refer to the whole group of people or things together, with no exceptions.

(87) Every member of the union was present.
'All members in the group were present without exceptions.'

Do not use *each* in negative statements.

(88) a. None of the students answered the essay question correctly.
b. *Each of the students didn't answer the essay question correctly.

Every can be modified, but not *each*.

(89) {Not every student, *Not each student} has a text.
'Some students have a text, and others do not.'

Quantified expressions such as {*some of, any of, each of*} take NPs.

(90) a. Here are some of [$_{NP}$ our regulations].
b. Do you have any of [$_{NP}$ the larger ones]?
c. Each (one) of [$_{NP}$ the answers] is worth 5 points.

Every of cannot take plural NPs, but *every one of* can.

(91) a. Every one of [$_{NP}$ the answers] is worth 5 points.
b. *Every of [$_{NP}$ the answers] is worth 5 points.

No one (= *no-one, nobody*) means *not anyone* or *no person*.

(92) a. Ross has three sons, but **no one** lives nearby.

b. **No one** can promise what the future holds for cancer patients, but today John is winning the fight against his particular form of cancer, enjoying a good quality of life and realizing his dreams.

None means *not one of a group of people or things*, or *not any*.

(93) a. Seven people became infected, but **none** died.

b. Lily and Marshall saw several houses, but **none** they really liked.

Exercise 5

5_1

Select the word that best completes each sentence:

(94) Platform is available to cast Republicans as protectors of (a, the) privileged at the expense of the middle class.

(95) A father helps his legally blind son climb (∅, the) Mount Kilimanjaro.

(96) A (custom, customs) agent might ask to see (∅, a) luggage.

(97) Wreckage of a WWII plane that crashed 70 years ago is found in (∅, a, the) Sahara Desert.

(98) Heavy rainstorms continue to hit (∅, a, the) east, central and southwest China.

(99) British historian Niall Ferguson looks at the changing economic dynamic and says the fact Europe has turned to China for help shows how drastically fortunes have reversed and (∅, a, the) mighty (has, have) fallen.

5_2

Underline every determiner in each sentence:

[e.g.] The bookstore is holding its annual textbook sale on Friday.

(100) My relatives have many odd habits.

(101) His youngest daughter keeps her pet in the kitchen.

(102) Other people sometimes have trouble with these weird antics.

5_3

Find errors and correct them in the following sentences:

(103) Let's go to a coffee shop at the corner of Bingfield Street.

(104) Nutritionists now believe that eating the soybeans may help stop calcium loss and prevent osteoporosis.

6 Adjectives

6.1 Usage

Attributive Usage

Most adjectives (As) appear in the following slot: +a, $[_{NP}$ Det (Num) ___ N].♣

(1) a. My decision to become a scholar was $[_{NP}$ a **smart** move].

b. I have won $[_{NP}$ the three **online** games].

Predicative Usage

Most As appear after linking Vs: +a, $[_{VP}$ V ___].

(2) a. Advertizing is **competitive**.

b. Joey is always **happy**.

♣ +a, $[_{NP}$ Det (Num) ___ N] is read as follows: A word whose POS is adjective appears in the underlined position which is followed by a noun and preceded by a determiner and an optional occurrence of number.

Some As appear **only** after linking Vs. They are inherently predicative.

(3) afraid, alive, alone, asleep, aware, content, due, glad, ill, ready, sorry, sure, unable, well

(4) a. The baby is asleep.

b. *the asleep baby

(5) a. The guy was clearly very content.

b. *the content guy

Some As must be used **only** as attributive modifiers. It means that they cannot be predicative.

(6) eastern, atomic, indoor, occasional, northern, countless, introductory, outdoor, southern, digital, maximum

(7) a. Professor Kim teaches an introductory course in linguistics.

b. *His teaching is introductory.

(8) a. He made occasional visits to Paris.

b. *His visit to Paris was occasional.

6.2 Ordering

+n, [NP (Det) (Num) ___ A]

Some As can be postmodifiers.

(9) a. The river is more than [sixty yards wide].

b. The walls are about [one meter thick].

c. the director **designate**

d. the president **elect**

e. At the flea market, there were [quilts, furniture, and books **galore**].

f. The media cast him as [the devil **incarnate**].

A few As may have different meanings depending on the position.

Meaning Difference

(10) a. The couple **concerned** gave the impression of being attracted to one another.
'involved in something'

b. He was much **concerned** about the question of the improvement of the clergy.
'worried about something'

(11) a. The plot was so **involved** that very few people knew what was going on.
'complicated'

b. The people **involved** are all doctors.
'being connected'

(12) a. I'm worried about the **present** situation.
'current, happening or existing now'

b. Of the 18 people **present**, I knew only one.
'in a particular place'

(13) a. Everything was in its **proper** place.
'right, suitable, or correct'

b. The friendly chat which comes before the interview **proper** is intended to relax the candidate.
'the real or main part of something'

(14) a. Children should be in the care of a **responsible** adult.
'sensible, reliable, trustworthy'

b. Who is **responsible** for this mess?
'blamed'

c. Police are determined to catch the man **responsible**.
'guilty, culpable'

Opinion - Descriptive

In theory, you can use As in any order. In practice, however, there is a normal order. For example, opinion As precede descriptive As.

(15) a. There are [two **nice little** places].

b. [Two **naughty little** children] are gone. [Three **good little** children] are left.

c. [The **beautiful creamy** paper] deserved to be written on with a real nib instead of being scratched with an ink-pencil.

SASCOM
(Size - Age - Shape - Color - Origin - Material)

There is a word order among descriptive As.

(16) a. a **large, young, hook-nosed** man with enormous forearms [size – age – shape]

b. They're a kind of [**round yellow** fruit with a thick skin]. [shape – color]

c. the **tiny wooden** dice [size – material]

d. Corelli sat at the table with [its **checked plastic** cloth]. [shape – material]

e. the **small round pink** bowl [size – shape – color]

f. the **new black HD** tablet [age – color – material]

Comparison As precede other As.

(17) a. Here are 5 secrets to [better French Toast] every time.

b. That is [the most dangerous small fish in the sea].

Among modifiers, adjectival modifiers precede nominal modifiers.

+n, [$_{NP}$ (D) (A) (N) ____]

(18) a. the traditional Italian pizza recipes

b. He observed the receipt for [his monthly cash payment].

6.3 Category-Selection

Some As may take *to* VPs or *that* clauses as their optional complements.

+a, [___ ({*to* VP, *that*-S})]

(19) afraid, anxious, ashamed, disappointed, frightened, glad, happy, pleased, proud, sad, surprised, unhappy

(20) a. We were proud to see them there.

b. We were proud that we saw them there.

(21) a. After more than 15 years in the States, she was anxious to spend more time with her aging parents in Sao Paulo.

b. Robin was anxious that Barney should meet her father.

Some As express an opinion, selecting *to* infinitives.

+a, [___ *to* VP]

(22) a. The little Greek horses carried their cavalry, and were too tough [to die].

b. It was a place impossible [to enter except on official business].

c. It was difficult [to keep track of them].

+a, [___ *that*-S]

Some As express an opinion, selecting *that* clauses.

(23) a. It was **essential** [**that** they should keep on going to the country].

b. Piggy and the parody were so **funny** [**that** the hunters began to laugh].

c. It's **obvious** [**that** everyone gets paid by the state].

+n, [___ *be* A ({*of, for*} NP) *to* VP]

Expletive *it* can be used as a fake subject, referring to the real subject realized as a *to* infinitive phrase.

(24) a. **It was** really **good of** him **to** give up the time.

b. **It's easy for** me **to** be his advocate.

-ing A

Many *-ing* As describe the effect that something has on your feelings.

(25) a. He let out the **amazing** truth.

b. all these **worrying** negotiations

-ed A

Many *-ed* As describe people's feelings.

(26) a. She was entirely **amazed** when her father did not even look up.

b. Frankly, I am quite **worried** about Tom.

Intensifiers such as {*quite, really, very*} may precede *-ing* and *-ed* As.

(27) a. That resemblance is **quite** strik**ing** when we examine the portrait of Simeon Lee as a young man.

b. He was **really** interest**ed** in books dealing with politics.

c. Life might be **very** amus**ing** in this world.

{*more, the most*} may precede -*ing* and -*ed* As.

(28) a. That was more terrifying than mere torture and death.

b. Any country which remained industrially backward was bound to be dominated by its more advanced rivals.

(29) a. It was the most affecting sight I have ever seen!

b. The most experienced and adroit painter could not by mere mechanical facility paint anything if the lines of the subject were not revealed to him first.

Some As obligatorily require *to* infinitive complements.♣

+a, [___ *to* VP]

(30) a. Winston was able *(to remain outside the range of the telescreen).

b. Wilcox is apt *(to be rather grudging when he is on his own).

c. Sooner or later they were bound *(to get you).

d. Possibly you are inclined *(to look at things too tragically).

e. The holding of debates was liable *(to bring him back).

f. Everything was likely *(to fall off her).

g. You are prepared *(to cheat, to forge, to blackmail, to corrupt the minds of children).

h. He was quite willing *(to do the selling for her).

♣ The star outside a parenthesis indicates that the parenthetical expression is mandatory.

Exercise 6

6_1

Select the expression that best completes each sentence:

(31) To simulate the experience of a (manning, manned) mission to Mars, a team of six will spend 520 days in windowless capsule.

(32) Rebecca Keegan talks about the rare circumstances (surrounding, surrounded) a recent (fundraising, fundraised) event for President Obama at the home of actor George Clooney.

(33) Gov. Mitt Romney gave the commencement address to (graduating, graduated) students at Liberty University on Saturday, where he had the opportunity to appeal to the stronghold of evangelical Christians.

(34) All of them would have been so much happier if they could have talked of the (forbidding, forbidden) topic of Richard.

(35) A website gathers the funniest of (those mistaken text messages, those text mistaken messages, mistaken those text messages) that make you laugh or turn red.

6_2

Put the words in parentheses in the right order to make sentences:

(36) The unequal distribution (Myanmar's, natural, enormous, of) wealth will continue to fuel conflict until there is some sort of political settlement.

(37) She must have crept in when we were all taken aback by the production of (stone, great, bloodstained, that, horrible).

(38) Oh, what (dinner, a, depressing, dismal) this was!

(39) On top of this, could he summon enough courage to crawl through (bored, straight, hole, a) through the base of a mountain?

7 Comparison

When Grammar Meets Linguistics

7.1 Form

-er, -est

{*-er*, *-est*} is attached to one-syllable As and Advs.

(1) a. old older oldest
b. fond fonder fondest
c. tall taller tallest
d. large larger largest

{*-r*, *-st*} is attached to one-syllable As and Advs which end in *-e*.

(2) a. safe safer safest
b. bare barer barest

Double the consonant when one-syllable As and Advs end in a single vowel and consonant (except -*w*).

(3)	a.	fit	fit**ter**	fit**test**
	b.	sad	sad**der**	sad**dest**
	c.	big	big**ger**	big**gest**
	d.	thin	thin**ner**	thin**nest**
(4)	a.	raw	raw**er**	raw**est**
	b.	slow	slow**er**	slow**est**

With two-syllable As and Advs ending in a consonant and -*y*, -*y* is changed to -*i*, and {-*er*, -*est*} is added.

(5)	a.	happy	happ**ier**	happ**iest**
	b.	drowsy	drows**ier**	drows**iest**
	c.	pretty	prett**ier**	prett**iest**

more, most

{*more, most*} is used for most two-syllable As, all longer As, and Advs ending in -*ly*. However, there are exceptions as in (7).

(6)	a.	useful	**more** useful	**most** useful
	b.	beautiful	**more** beautiful	**most** beautiful
	c.	seriously	**more** seriously	**most** seriously
(7)	a.	early	earl**ier**	earl**iest**
	b.	friendly	friendl**ier**	friendl**iest**
	c.	lovely	lovel**ier**	lovel**iest**

less, least

Less and *least* make comparisons with the opposite meaning to *more* and *most*.

(8) a. He was **less** frightened **than** he would normally have been.

b. I don't see **the least** chance of it.

Irregular

Irregular forms for comparison are the following:

(9)	a.	good/well	better	best
	b.	bad/badly	worse	worst
	c.	far	farther/further	farthest/furthest
	d.	old	older/elder	oldest/eldest
	e.	many/much	more	most
	f.	little	less	least
	g.	late	later/latter	latest/last

Descriptive Gr

Nowadays, people usually say *further* rather than *farther*, and *furthest* rather than *farthest*. Below, *further* and *furthest* may mean either *degree* or *distance*.

(10) a. There were **further** angry demonstrations. [degree]

b. But he did not pursue the thought **further**. [degree]

c. Now he had retreated a step **further**. [distance]

d. There was a vacant place at a table **further** away. [distance]

(11) a. The Athenians progressed **furthest** towards developing a truly democratic society. [degree]

b. The **furthest** limit of his sufferings was still unchanged.[degree]

c. She went to the furthest end of the little drawing room and sank into a low chair. [distance]

d. How long does it take you to get to the furthest point? [distance]

7.2 Comparative Usage

Inequality comparisons may express superiority or inferiority relationships. Comparative As usually accompany *than*.

(12) a. A column of men, much smarter than most of the others, marched by in unison.

b. Those who were with him were fewer than those on the other side of the wall.

Degree adverbials modify comparative As.

(13) a. She knows it a bit more clearly than he.

b. With just a few dabs of color in the right places, she had become not only very much prettier, but, above all, far more feminine.

c. He had some connection with an insurance office which made the arrangement slightly less painful to him.

The pattern of [*the* comparative A ... , *the* comparative A ...] amounts to saying that one situation depends on another.

(14) a. The sooner the better.

b. The offering must be made, and the harder it was to make, the more valuable it must be in his eyes.

c. Similarly, the more examples a writer provides, the more compelling are the writer's conclusions.

d. Classes are sometimes criticized because there is too much TTT (Teacher Talking Time) and not enough STT (Student Talking Time). Overuse of TTT is inappropriate because the more a teacher talks, the less chance there is for the students to practice their own speaking—and it is the students who need the practice, not the teacher.

The pattern of [comparative A *and* comparative A] indicates that something increases or decreases.

(15) a. It gets worse and worse the further we go.

b. The aim of establishing liberty and equality was more and more openly abandoned.

c. Mary was finding it harder and harder to get sleep.

7.3 Superlative Usage

The superlative As or Advs in a sentence choose a specific person or thing among all members of a group. Superlative As usually accompany a Det such as *the* or possessives.

(16) Wonka's chocolate factory is the biggest in the world.

(17) a. I was wearing my oldest pajamas.

b. Her unmarried oldest sister is equally vain.

c. Like a taunting silhouette emerging from the fog, the branches of Britain's oldest apple tree burgeoned with five-petaled blossoms, all glistening like Venus.

Degree adverbials modify [*the* + superlative As].

(18) a. Snowball and Napoleon were by far the most active in the debates.

b. The vehicle was easily the smallest car Langdon had ever seen.

c. You may find that you could get there by plane. If so, that's much the easiest.

d. Scarlett thought it quite the ugliest dwelling she had ever seen.

In the pattern of [superlative A + (NP) + PP], the PP restricts the range of the group.

(19) a. He slipped into the nearest [of them] as inconspicuously as he could.

b. Her turban was twice as large as the largest [of any of the others].

c. The Nile is the longest river [in Africa] and the second in length [of all the rivers of the globe].

d. The Irish are the poorest liars [in the world].

Prescriptive Gr

According to Prescriptive Grammar, *least* appears before non-countable Ns, and *fewest* before countable Ns.

(20) a. As these examples show, Brainard presents his memories in a consistently flat, factual manner, eschewing commentary or the least smile of irony.

b. The rockin' 28-year-old teacher was revealed to have received **the fewest viewer votes** Thursday on the Fox singing competition.

7.4 Equality Comparison

Equality comparisons describe two things as being similar by way of *as* ... *as*.

as {A, Adv} *as* XP

(21) a. The urge to shout filthy words at the top of his voice was **as strong as** ever.

b. He sat **as still as** a mouse.

c. It was **as instinctive** to them **as** teaching was to me.

Some Advs modify equality comparisons.

(22) a. The wave of pain receded **almost** as quickly as it had come.

b. Mr. Wonka was clearly **just** as excited as everybody else.

c. It was certainly carried **nearly** as far as possible.

d. I remember times when it was **quite** as hot as this in Malaya.

The same as means *exactly like*.

(23) a. A peace that was truly permanent would be **the same as** a permanent war.

b. He was doing **the same as** everyone did.

The same means *very similar*.

(24) a. I know it is **the same** with them all.

b. We'll see to it that the people who get elected are **the same** people who were on the ad hoc committee.

c. According to a new poll, 55 percent of those surveyed believe the economy will get better under Mitt Romney, but only 46 percent said **the same** of President Barack Obama.

Some Advs may modify the sequence of [*the same*].

(25) a. I said **exactly** the same to him.

b. It seems to me they are all **more or less** the same thing.

c. She felt **much** the same emotions.

d. I heard **almost** the same thing once before from someone very different.

e. But I went ahead and did it **just** the same.

The pattern of [linking V + *like* α] is used to indicate equality comparisons.

(26) a. They **were like** the ant, which can see small objects but not large ones.

b. It **smells like** rubbing alcohol.

Exercise 7

7_1

Select the expression that best completes each sentence:

(27) Murphy's Oil Soap is the chemical (more, most) commonly used to clean elephants.

(28) If things get any (worse, worst), I'll have to ask you to stop helping me.

(29) Did you hear about my new boyfriend? He's not the (sharper, sharpest) tool in the shed.

(30) Good advice: Love (deep, deeply) and (passionate, passionately). You might get hurt, but it's the only way to live life completely.

(31) Doctor: "You're coughing (easier, easiest) today."
Patient: "No wonder. I practiced all night."

7_2

Find ill-formed modifiers and correct them in the following sentences:

[e.g.] Which is the most famous Russian ballet company, the Kirov or the Bolshoi?

[Answer: Which is *the more* famous Russian ballet company, the Kirov or the Bolshoi?]

(32) When Barbara-Rose Collins served as a state representative in Michigan, my aunt thought that she fought harder than any representative for key legislation to help minorities.

(33) Lucia has the most uncommonest hobby I've ever heard of—collecting insects.

(34) The night before last, the worse snowstorm ever to hit the metropolitan area swept in from the frigid seas of the Arctic.

(35) Of the three tennis teams, our partnership is the more nearly equal.

8 Adverbials

When Grammar Meets Linguistics

POS

The part of speech (POS) of adverbials is diverse.

(1) a. He ran [$_{\text{Adv}}$ **slowly**].

b. He ran [$_{\text{AdvP}}$ **very slowly**].

c. He ran [$_{\text{PP}}$ **in a slow manner**].

d. He ran [$_{\text{NP}}$ **every night**].

Classification

The types of adverbials are diverse: manner, place, and time adverbials. They usually follow Vs.

(2) a. At last the lobby was **reasonably** quiet. [manner]

b. One of them was a girl whom he often passed **in the corridors**. [place]

c. We will arrange something else for you **later**. [time]

Ordering

Within VP, an adverbial cannot intervene between a V and its object NP: [$_{VP}$ V NP adverbial].

(3) a. I have plainly [$_{VP}$ bored all the students **into condition of coma**].

b *I have plainly [$_{VP}$ bored **into condition of coma** all the students].

There is a word order among adverbials: [manner - place - time].

(4) She danced **elegantly** **at the ball** **last night**.

{Frequency, probability, duration, degree} adverbials precede main Vs.

(5) a. She **often** talked about the need for teamwork among her peers.

b. The message **probably** meant death.

c. At the table on his left, the man with the strident voice was **still** talking remorselessly away.

d. The story **really** began in the mid-sixties.

S-adverbial

Adverbials may appear sentence-initially. They are called sentential adverbials.

(6) a. **Slowly** they began to limp back towards the farm.

b. **At those moments** his secret loathing of Big Brother changed into adoration.

Adverbial - V - S

Fronted adverbials may induce the inversion of subjects and Auxes (or Vs).

(7) a. **Next to it** was a toy shop.

b. **Never again** will you be capable of ordinary human feelings.

c. **Little** does she know the health problems result from her premature delivery after her birth mother attempted to abort her.

Manner adverbials are formed in the following way: manner Adv = A + *ly*.

Manner

(8) a. rugged ruggedly
b. slow slowly
c. natural naturally
d. abrupt abruptly
e. cautious cautiously

Note that if the suffix -*ly* is attached to an N, an A is derived: A = N + *ly*.

(9) a. **ecofriendly** motorbikes
b. Ross gave me a **comradely** slap on the back.

There may be changes in spelling.

(10) a. simple simply
b. full fully
c. heavy heavily
d. mechanical mechanically

Some manner Advs and As are morphologically identical.

(11) a. She knew all those **fast** American dances. [= quick]
b. He cannot run **fast** enough to catch rabbits. [= quickly]

However, note the following contrast.

(12) a. With no clocks and no daylight, it was **hard** to gauge the time. [= difficult]

b. I had **hardly** thought about it. [= almost not, certainly not]

(13) a. She was **late** for work every morning. [= after the planned time]

b. What treasure have you been buying **lately** at the old curiosity shops? [= recently]

Manner adverbials are realized as {PP, NP, *like* NP}.

(14) a. He began writing **in a hurried untidy scrawl**.

b. The process was all-or-nothing; either you failed to modify at all, or else you modified **the whole way**.

c. You saw him wallowing along in the water **like a porpoise**.

8.1 Time Adverbials

Time adverbials may be represented by NPs.

(15) last night, next week, the day after tomorrow, the other day, today, yesterday

Time NP adverbials do not need Ps such as {*at, on, in*}.

(16) a. Bernard asked me to meet the Savage **next Wednesday**.

b. *Bernard asked me to meet the Savage **on next Wednesday**.

The present tense may indicate the future time, along with time adverbials.

(17) a. After a double overtime game I think it's better to rest and try to recover and **come** back ready to go **tomorrow**.

b. He's going to drive me home when I **go** home **next month**.

The PPs composed of [*at* NP] may be used as time adverbials.

(18) a. at about 10:30 a.m. [clock times]

b. at a Hindu festival, at Easter [religious festivals]

c. at breakfast, at lunchtimes [meal times]

d. at dawn, at the weekend [specific periods]

The PPs composed of [*in* NP] may be used as time adverbials.

(19) a. in summer [seasons]

b. in 1997, in the 21st century [years and centuries]

c. in January [months]

d. in the afternoon [parts of the day]

The PPs composed of [*on* NP] may be used as time adverbials.

(20) a. on Monday, on Tuesday morning [days]

b. on Christmas Day, on my birthday [special days]

c. on the eleventh of January, on November 5th [dates]

For is used to show an amount of time.

(21) a. You might dodge successfully **for a while**.

b. **For a week** after this, life was like a restless dream.

In the pattern of [... V ... *since* ...], the V takes the present perfect or past perfect tense in order to indicate a particular time in the past until now or a later time.

(22) a. You must **have seen** great changes **since** you were a young man.

b. Four days **had gone** past **since** the evening when he had run into her outside the junk-shop.

During means 'at some point in a period of time,' or 'through the whole of a period of time.'

(23) a. People simply disappeared, always **during the night**.

b. Intel has developed an application called Mobile Therapy that pops up randomly and asks users to record their mood, to see how it varies **during the week**.

Over means 'at one point' or 'at various different points during a period of time.'

(24) a. I'm going to redecorate my bedroom **over the holidays**.

b. The number of mosques has nearly doubled **over the past decade**.

[*From ... to/till/until*] or [*between ... and*] is used for the beginning and end of a period of time.

(25) a. The Youth League surrounded the courts **from** morning **to** night, chanting at intervals "Death to the traitors!"

b. The diggers worked **from** dawn **till** dusk.

c. Apart from this brief period, the island was Venetian **from** 1194 **until** 1797.

(26) There is no difference **between** night **and** day in this place.

By means 'before or not later than a particular time.'

(27) a. He had to be back at work **by** fourteen-thirty.

b. **By** the third day, his eyes ached unbearably and his spectacles needed wiping every few minutes.

8.2 Frequency Adverbials and Probability Adverbials

Frequency

Frequency adverbials are the adverbials showing the number of times that something happens within a particular period of time.

(28) a lot, always, ever, frequently, hardly ever, never, normally, occasionally, often, rarely, sometimes, usually

(29) a. She began to be more and more **frequently** aware of those joys.

b. In these days Napoleon **rarely** appeared in public, but spent all his time in the farmhouse.

Probability

Probability adverbials are adverbials showing how likely something is.

(30) certainly, definitely, maybe, obviously, perhaps, possibly, probably, really

(31) a. She had **certainly** turned very pale.

b. **Perhaps** it was for corruption or incompetence.

+adv, [{ ___ V, Λux/*be* ___ }]

Frequency or probability adverbials are placed before {main Vs} or after {auxiliaries, *be*}.

(32) a. People with dark hair **sometimes** have blue eyes.

b. A roll will **sometimes** smell so good (that) one can't resist it.

c. He's a very nervous man, and is **sometimes** out of humor.

+adv, [{ ___ S, S ___ }]

Perhaps may be used as a sentential Adv.

(33) a. **Perhaps** a quarter of the windows in the street were broken.

b. A quarter of the windows in the street were broken, **perhaps**.

+adv, [___ V]

Never is a negative adverbial. It precedes main Vs.

(34) a. Such incidents **never** had any sequel.

b. He did not exist: he had **never** existed.

Ever is used in questions, negative sentences, or *if* clauses.

(35) a. Has he **ever** been here alone**?**

b. Do**n't** **ever** tell anybody anything.

c. **If** we **ever** hated them, it was with affection and even gratitude in our hearts.

8.3 Duration Adverbials

Duration adverbials indicate the length of time that something continues.

(36) a. The day was **still** cold and clear.

b. I didn't think it had been issued **yet**.

c. No, thanks, I can't drink **any more**.

The duration adverbial *already* cannot be used in negative statements but can be in negative *if* clauses.

(37) a. *He **hadn't already** bribed the magistrates and police.

b. **If** I **hadn't already** resolved to run away, I'm sure I would have been terrified to think of the suffering that probably lay in wait for me in Gion.

Still is used for saying that a situation continues to exist up to a particular time, or that something remains true despite what you have just done or said.

(38) a. Ted may not approve of what Marshall did, but Marshall is **still** Ted's best friend.

b. The animals knew that this was not the case. **Still**, it had been decided to build the walls three feet thick this time instead of eighteen inches as before, which meant collecting much larger quantities of stone.

The duration adverbial *yet* may appear at the end of negative statements and questions.

(39) a. I did**n't** think it had been issued **yet**.

b. Hasn't he gone into the country **yet?**

Usage

Not any {*longer, more*} is used for saying that somebody has stopped doing something, or a situation has ended. *No* {*longer, more*} sounds formal.

(40) a. Oceania was **not any longer** at war with Eurasia.

b. They did**n't** pay **any more** attention to him.

(41) a. Oceania was **no longer** at war with Eurasia.

b. They paid **no more** attention to him.

8.4 Degree Adverbials

+adv, [{ ___ V}, {V (NP) ___ }]

The following degree adverbials may appear in a preverbal or post-verbal position.

(42) badly, greatly, strongly, completely, seriously, totally

(43) a. The tales about Frederick's cruelty had been **greatly exaggerated**.

b. The tales about Frederick's cruelty had been **exaggerated greatly**.

(44) a. He is **seriously considering** face-lift.

b. He is **considering** face-lift **seriously**.

+adv, [___ V]

The following degree adverbials typically appear before Vs.

(45) almost, largely, nearly, really, quite

(46) It's all over and done with now, and **nearly forgotten**.

Really is a sentential adverbial.

+adv, [{ ___ S, S ___ }]

(47) a. Really, he's getting quite a man.

b. He's getting quite a man, really.

{*a lot, very much*} appears in the clause-final position.

+adv, [$_{VP}$ V (NP) ___]

(48) a. The bishop and I walk a lot.

b. I didn't care for them very much.

The following degree adverbials are premodifiers.

+adv, [___ {A, Adv}]

(49) awfully, fairly, quite, really, extremely, pretty, rather, very

(50) a. I am awfully fond of it.

b. I am awfully deeply fond of it.

The position of *rather* is a bit flexible: [___ *a*(*n*) A N] or [*a* ___ A N].

rather

(51) a. He's a very remarkable man; rather a conservative, but a splendid man.

b. He's a very remarkable man; a rather conservative, but splendid man.

In (52a) *quite* means *fairly*: [___ *a*(*n*) A N]. In (52b) *quite* means *extremely*: [*a* ___ A N].

quite

(52) a. Nevertheless, I found him quite a shrewd man, very well able to appreciate the somewhat intricate points that came up about the lease and his capital improvements.

b. There was a sort of calculating ferocity in the boy's eye, a quite evident desire to hit or kick Winston.

+adv, [___ {S, PP}]

The following adverbials are premodifiers.

(53) entirely, just, largely, mainly, partly, simply

(54) a. Calpurnia always won, mainly because Atticus always took her side.

b. Langdon was grateful simply for the opportunity to meet him.

so, such

So and *such* are degree modifiers which emphasize a quality that somebody or something has: [*so* {A, Adv}] and [*such* (*a*(*n*)) (A) N].

(55) a. When you looked at O'Brien's powerful shoulders and his blunt-featured face, so ugly and yet so civilized, it was impossible to believe that he could be defeated.

b. It emptied his lungs so completely that he could only begin breathing again by lying on his back and taking a series of deep gasps.

(56) a. Consider, for example, such a typical sentence from a Times leading article.

b. Such incidents never had any sequel.

too, enough

Too and *enough* are degree adverbials. Note their syntactic position: *too* is a premodifier, and *enough* a postmodifier.

(57) a. The impact that it had made on everyone's eyeballs was too vivid to wear off immediately.

b. He knew very well the danger of showing too much interest.

(58) a. Your portfolio today must be more dynamic—flexible enough to adapt to rapidly changing markets—and more diverse than it's ever been before.

b. He could evade its pangs if he was quick-witted enough.

Det *enough*

Enough can be used as a Det as in (59). In (60a) *dirty* is clearly an A. The ungrammaticality of (60b) suggests that *enough* and *dirty* have a different status regarding the modification of the head N *money*. In (61) *the* is clearly a Det. The mutual exclusiveness of *the* and *enough* in (61) confirms that *enough* is a sort of Dets.

(59) Have we [$_{NP}$ enough chairs]?

(60) a. enough dirty money

b. *dirty enough money

(61) a. *the enough money

b. *enough the money

Intensifier

The following shows emphasizing adverbials (= intensifiers).

(62) absolutely, completely, entirely, perfectly, purely, quite, really, simply, totally, utterly

(63) He had pulled her down on to the ground, and she was utterly unresisting.

8.5 Free Adjuncts

S-adverbial

Sentential adjuncts are usually introduced by a subordinator such as *while, if,* or *whether*, which determines their semantic relationship with the main clause. Free adjuncts are sentence-level adverbials which do not have an overt conjunction linking them to the main clause (cf. Quirk et al. 1985). They express a proposition that is semantically subordinate to the proposition expressed by the main clause.

Attendant Circumstance

Free adjuncts express attendant circumstances: concurrent action as in (64), sequential action as in (65), reason as in (66), instrument as in (67), and condition as in (68).

Concurrent

(64) Going into the hall, he saw a handsome groom, in a braided livery and a bear fur cape, holding a white fur cloak.
'While he went into the hall, ...'

Sequential

(65) Going into the shady outer room, he took down from the wall his veil, that hung on a peg, and putting it on, and thrusting his hands into his pockets.
'After he went into the shady outer room, ...'

Reason

(66) Merthin smiled faintly, guessing that she had maneuvered herself into this position.
'... because she guessed that she had maneuvered herself into this position'

(67) **Pushing himself up**, he staggered on, feeling angry and desperate inside.
'By pushing himself up, ...'

Instrument

(68) **Supposing that it could be somehow resurrected from its ashes**, the photograph might not even be evidence.
'Even if we suppose that it could be ...'

Condition

After the main clause, free adjuncts are used for giving information or elaborating on the content in the main clause.

Elaboration

(69) a. "Oh bastard," the Judge murmured, and pulled his hand out of Roberts's rain-slippery grip just as Roberts fired through the pocket of his slicker. The bullet ploughed through the Judge's midsection just below the stomach, **flattening, spinning, mushrooming, coming out to the right of his spine, leaving an exit hole the size of a tea saucer**.

b. He was everywhere at once, **pushing, pulling, sawing, hammering, improvising, jollying everyone along with comradely exhortations**.

Exercise 8

8_1

Underline every adverbial in each sentence, and then write every word modified by each adverbial:

[e.g.] The people often have noisy parties on the weekends.

[Answer: The people <u>often</u> have noisy parties <u>on the weekends</u>. They modify *have*.]

(70) Several friends are coming to my apartment on Saturday night for a party.

(71) In this part of the country, we often have exciting thunderstorms on summer evenings.

(72) How do people in the far north live happily in winter with so few hours of daylight?

(73) A counter job at a fast-food restaurant will probably not make anyone rich.

8_2

The grammatical function of adverbials is operated by Advs, PPs, NPs, VPs, or clauses. Underline every adverbial in each sentence, and then write the POS of each adverbial:

[e.g.] Last night the wind was blowing hard.

[Answer: <u>Last night</u> (NP) the wind was blowing <u>hard</u> (AdvP)].

(74) My father moved to Florida last year when he retired.

(75) To get to work on Monday, I caught the early train.

(76) When you take the stairs, your legs lift the entire weight for your body at every step.

8_3

Probably is a sentential adverbial. Identify two other sentential adverbials from the list. [List: *completely, partially, clearly, incorrectly, stupidly, carelessly, obviously*]

(77) a. Probably Mary has solved the problem.

b. Mary probably has solved the problem.

c. Mary has probably solved the problem.

d. cf. It is probable that Mary has solved the problem.

Lolly, Lolly, Lolly, Get Your Adverbs Here

[Words and Music by Bob Dorough]

Lolly Lolly Lolly, get your adverbs here!
Lolly Lolly Lolly, got some adverbs here!
Come on down to Lolly's, get the adverbs here!
You're going to need
If you write or read
Or even think about it.

Lolly Lolly Lolly, get your adverbs here!
Got a lot of Lolly, jolly adverbs here!
Anything you need
And we can make it absolutely clear!

An adverb is a word ... {That's all it is, and there's a lot of 'em!}
That modifies a verb ... {Sometimes a verb! Sometimes ...}
It modifies an adjective,
Or else another adverb.
And so you see that it's positively, very, very, necessary.

Lolly Lolly Lolly, get your adverbs here!
Father, son and Lolly selling adverbs here!
Got a lot of adverbs and we make it clear,
So come to Lolly!

9 Prepositions

9.1 Prepositional Phrases (PPs)

Prepositions (Ps) appear as the head of a prepositional phrase (PP), usually followed by an object NP.

PP

(1) a. On Saturday evening, the Des Moines Register released a poll showing a highly volatile race.

b. Prices may vary in areas outside metropolitan Washington.

The string of [P NP P] is often analyzed as an idiomatic expression where a P is followed by an NP which is followed by another P.

[$_{PP}$ P NP P NP]

(2) a. His presence signals the Obama campaign's determination not to be drowned out by the GOP race and to use whatever platform is available to cast Republicans as protectors of the privileged [$_{PP}$ at the expense of the middle class].

b. Four years after trading Carlos Quentin from Arizona to the Chicago White Sox, new Padres General Manager Josh Byrnes is bringing the all-star outfielder back home to San Diego [$_{PP}$ **in a trade with** the White Sox].

[$_{PP}$ P NP *that*-S]

In the following, PPs have a complex structure of [$_{PP}$ P NP *that*-S]. *That* clauses are used as noun-complement clauses.

(3) a. One senior official, speaking [$_{PP}$ **on the condition that** he not be identified], noted that his strategists would have expected Democrats to seize on that argument anyway.

b. The Oversight Committee chairman asked whether the agency has made plans [$_{PP}$ **in the event that** Cordray's nomination is invalidated by a legal appeal].

[$_{PP}$ P [$_{PP}$ P NP]]

Ps such as *from* or *down* may be immediately followed by another P.

(4) a. And then, the next minute, I saw the gray outlines of rocks gradually appearing [$_{PP}$ **from behind** the clouds].

b. Even the stubborn unemployment rate ticked [$_{PP}$ **down below** 9 percent] at the end of 2011.

P A

[P A] strings often have meanings similar to Advs.

(5) a. in private = privately

b. in vain = vainly

c. in full = fully

d. of late = lately

(6) a. No interest if paid **in full** within 24 months with your credit card.

b. Adding to its woes, Hungary has been in a standoff **of late** with international financial institutions over a new law that reduces the independence of its central bank.

9.2 Thematic Roles

Thematic roles are assigned to object NPs by Vs or Ps in order to indicate their meaning relation in a clause.

Location

Ps such as *in*, *on*, *under*, or *beside* indicate a place.

(7) a. Syria has shot down a Turkish military jet **in** Syrian airspace; now both countries are looking for the missing pilots.

b. Militant Islamists pitted against a guerrilla militia with grand ambitions to stage an attack **on** U.S. soil.

c. A thin layer of molten heavy elements including uranium and potassium still burbled just **under** the crust.

d. A bomb that seriously injured a Colorado couple was left **beside** their car **in** a paper bag with their names written **on** it.

Source

Ps such as *from*, *off*, or *amid* indicate an action's point of origin.

(8) a. We are surrounded **from** every direction.

b. The upshot is that the length of the paths of rays of light entering the silver, bouncing **off** the mirror, and then returning to the outside world (and so to the viewer) can be changed by varying the angle of tilt.

c. Thousands of Egyptians pack Tahrir Square **amid** reports that Ahmed Shafik could be named president Sunday.

Goal Ps such as *to*, *into*, or *onto* indicate an action's point of termination.

(9) a. We are making several enhancements **to** *The Washington Post* aimed at improving navigation and showcasing some of our most widely read content.

b. His wife spotted one of Lily's daughters walking **into** the restaurant.

c. In a year of global protests, few were as broadly backed as India's mass movement against corruption, which drew millions of people **into** the streets and **onto** social media to express support for veteran activist Anna Hazare as he staged a series of hunger strikes.

Instrument Ps such as *with* or *by* describe a tool or an instrument which is used for performing an action.

(10) a. Instantly his face turned scarlet and the water ran out of his eyes. The stuff was like nitric acid, and moreover, in swallowing it one had the sensation of being hit on the back of the head **with** a rubber club.

b. His hair was very fair, his face naturally sanguine, his skin roughened **by** coarse soap and blunt razor blades and the cold of the winter that had just ended.

Comitative Ps such as *with* express accompaniment.

(11) Winston Smith, his chin nuzzled into his breast in an effort to escape the vile wind, slipped quickly through the glass doors of Victory Mansions, though not quickly enough to prevent a swirl of gritty dust from entering along **with** him.

9.3 Time, Place, and Direction Prepositions

Place → Time

All Ps have a meaning of time, place, or direction. Some Ps of place may refer to time.

(12) a. Firefighters quickly put out a car fire **at** about 6 p.m.

b. For installed sales, retainers must be taken **by** 1/2/12. Sales must be completed **by** 1/15/12. Offer good **thru** 1/2/12.

c. It is a shift that reflects a double-digit drop in killings in the District **from** 2010 **to** 2011, with an especially noticeable downward trend in the most stubborn crime zones east of the Anacostia River.

Place

The following shows place Ps.

(13) above, among, at, behind, below, beneath, beside, between, by, in, inside, near, on, opposite, outside, over, round, through, under, underneath

(14) a. Is Dave sitting {**beside**, **by**} you?

b. Stealthy ultra-light aircraft bombed the lettuce fields **outside** town with bundles of dope, then swoop back into Mexico, well below radar but high {**above**, **over**} the fence.

The following shows phrasal place Ps.

(15) in between, in front of, next to, on top of

(16) a. The questions correspond to what I call the four basic spans of a job: control, accountability, influence, and support. Each span can be adjusted so that it is narrow or wide or somewhere **in between**.

b. Is Dave sitting **next to** you?

Direction The following shows direction Ps.

(17) across, along, back to, down, into, onto, out of, past, round, through, to, towards, up

(18) a. The case of Chen Guangcheng has brought new attention **to** China's Human Right's record and U.S. attempts to nudge Beijing **towards** reform.

b. They sent the problem **back to** their bosses.

Place and/or Direction The following illustrates Ps which can be used for place and/or direction.

(19) a. Waistlines are expanding **across** the globe.

b. Migrants and smugglers could slip through the alfalfa fields outside town or plow their pickup trucks through the desert, where the biggest worries were stuck tires and getting safely **across** the irrigation canals.

(20) a. Today, they rule **over** significant territory in this strategic region, near important oil shipping lanes.

b. Better yet, Luis said, for $3,000 a guide will take you **over** the fence and through the desert at night, and $6,000 buys a legitimate U.S. visa rented from a look alike with legal status.

POS What is the POS of the shaded?

(21) a. He had given a quick glance up and [$_{P}$ **down**] the street and then had slipped inside and bought the book for two dollars fifty.

b. Winston took up his mug of gin, paused for an instant to collect his nerve, and gulped the oily-tasting stuff [$_{Adv}$ **down**].

(22) a. She could see horses standing [$_P$ underneath] the trees, swishing long black tails.

b. 'If it's buried it's going to be all rotten and broken, isn't it?' 'I don't think so. There was a big trapdoor in the middle of the floor, and it was in a hole [$_{Adv}$ underneath].'

Note the contrast between place *at* and *in*.

at, in

(23) a. On Wednesday he appeared at the office after a week at home, and Leona Cassiani was horrified at seeing him so pale and enervated.
'*At* emphasizes the office as a public place or institution.'

b. On a cold January afternoon in 1866, Scarlett sat in the office writing a letter to Aunt Pitty, explaining in detail for the tenth time why neither she, Melanie nor Ashley could come back to Atlanta to live with her.
'*In* emphasizes the office as a building.'

(24) a. She had spent the morning at the library, reading up on gardening. Nor was she the only student. She saw two or three people with books on farming, a bespectacled young man of about twenty five poring over a book called *Seven Independent Power Sources for Your Home*, and a pretty blond girl of about fourteen with a battered paperback titled *600 Simple Recipes*.
'*At* emphasizes the library as a public place.'

b. He would never love me because of Rebecca. She was in the house still, as Mrs. Danvers had said; she was in that room in the west wing, she was in the library, in the morning-room, in the gallery above the hall. Even in the little flower-room, where her mackintosh still hung. And in the garden, and in the woods, and down in the stone cottage on the beach.
'*In* emphasizes the library as a building.'

GF — The complement of a P functions as either the subject or object of derived action nominals such as *reaction* or *destruction*.

(25) a. I believed the reaction [$_{PP}$ of the police officers] was excessive. [GF = Subject]

b. He said he was looking forward to sailing down the Amazon, where the group aims to highlight the destruction [$_{PP}$ of tropical rainforests]. [GF = Object]

9.4 Category-Selection: [$_{AP}$ A [$_{PP}$ P NP]]

+a, [___ (PP)] — The following A **may** take a PP.

(26) He was afraid (of the indiscriminate bombings by security forces).

+a, [___ PP] — The following A **must** take a PP.

(27) a. I think he was aware *(of what he had been through).

b. By now, many Metro riders are accustomed *(to delays, confusion and a lack of information, so they're in no mood to be patient).

c. But these are offset by the fact that every character in this novel, save the villains, is physically beautiful, morally upright, carefully tailored and overly fond *(of discussing Catholic theology and the works of Erik Satie).

+a, [___ (*of* NP)] — Some As may take [*of* NP] as their complement.

(28) afraid, ashamed, convinced, critical, envious, frightened, jealous, proud, scared, suspicious, terrified, tired

(29) a. No matter how much he claims otherwise, the fact is that few people are **envious of** Romney's business success.

b. Fellow musicians seemed enthused if not exactly **envious**.

Some As may take [*to* NP] as their complement.

+a, [___ (*to* NP)]

(30) close, dedicated, devoted, engaged, equal, identical, loyal, married, related, similar

(31) a. They see him as a man of high morals **devoted to** his family and experienced in the private sector, but also as someone disconnected from their lives by his wealth and background.

b. This work seems to mean much to her. I'm sure she'll give a performance which is **devoted** and emotional but never sentimental.

Some As may take [*with* NP] as their complement.

+a, [___ (*with* NP)]

(32) bored, content, displeased, dissatisfied, impatient, impressed, pleased, satisfied

(33) a. Not everyone was **impressed with** the way the Redskins handled the players' final day at the team facility.

b. They arrived just in time for the playoffs and everyone was really **impressed**.

Some As may take [*at* NP] as their complement.

+a, [___ (*at* NP)]

(34) alarmed, amazed, astonished, bad, excellent, good, hopeless, shocked, surprised, useless

(35) a. Those critics now want Mr. Stanley's head, or rather his job. In fact, removing him would be a piteous overreaction, for Mr. Stanley, whatever his shortcomings as a diplomat, is a nationally renowned planner, and **excellent at** his job.

b. I forgot to say that Chrysostom, who is dead, was a great man for writing verses, so much so that he made carols for Christmas Eve, and plays for Corpus Christi, which the young men of our village acted, and all said they were **excellent**.

+a, [___ (*for* NP)]

Some As may take [*for* NP] as their complement.

(36) common, difficult, easy, essential, important, necessary, possible, usual

(37) a. But what makes Tebow loved by his coaches and teammates is that it isn't just talk. It is an authentic personal piety that can build qualities **essential for** footbal success: courage, coolness under pressure, leadership, servanthood.

b. Much more education for Members of Congress about the workings of the Internet is **essential**.

The following As are used in three different ways.

(38) cruel, friendly, gracious, generous, good, kind, mean, nasty, nice, polite, rude

(39) a. You were **nice**.

b. It was **nice of** you **to** talk to me.

c. You were **nice** to me **for** no reason.

(40) a. These events perfect date nights where the pours of wine are **generous** and the food pairings, though small, can be downright stunning.

b. It would be gracious and generous of your department to recognize that both women are about to have babies.

c. Col. Gaboury was generous with his time for others, and always made time to counsel or console anyone in need.

9.5 Category-Selection: $[_{VP}$ V $[_{PP}$ P NP]]

The following Vs may take [*about* NP]. +v, [___ (*about* NP)]

(41) care, complain, dream, explain, hear, know, speak, talk, think

(42) a. Smith is merely trying to explain about how counter-productive it is.

b. In the Broncos' locker room, Tebow picked at his snack and tried to explain.

The following Vs may take [*at* NP]. +v, [___ (*at* NP)]

(43) glance, glare, laugh, look, shout, smile, stare

(44) a. I enjoy the research. Children stare at me in disbelief when they hear that, but the research is my excuse to talk to people I wouldn't otherwise meet, to take excursions to places that are off the beaten track, and to read in depth on fascinating subjects.

b. She tried not to stare.

The following Vs may take [*for* NP]. +v, [___ (*for* NP)]

(45) apologize, apply, ask, look, wait

(46) a. He wants to apply for a loan so he can expand his operation again.

b. Those were old regulations which don't apply any more.

+v, [___ (*into* NP)]

The following Vs may take [*into* NP].

(47) crash, drive, run

(48) a. If a second moon did crash into the first, the collision would have occurred when the big moon was young and hot.

b. And if we have to go through an unplanned transition, all the hard work you've done could go out the window. The stock could crash.

+v, [___ (*of* NP)]

The following Vs may take [*of* NP].

(49) hear, know, speak, talk, think

(50) a. This "too pure to win on the world's terms" ethos is deeply ingrained in conservative culture, not to speak of Catholicism.

b. Every time I speak, I say how important it is to ignore, or at least carefully filter, outside advice.

+v, [___ *on* NP]

The following Vs **must** take [*on* NP].

(51) count, depend, rely

(52) But Assad's bluster appears to be rooted in confidence that he can count on Russia, and perhaps China, to veto any U.N. resolution that would call for tougher action.

The following Vs may take a variety of categories as their complement: *to* NP, NP, *that* clause, or wh-clause.

+v, [___ {*to* NP, NP, *that*-S, wh-S}]

(53) complain, explain, listen, say, speak, talk, write

(54) a. I am angry over these reactions and am wondering how to **explain to** people better than I already had about how their reactions are inconsiderate.

b. She must continually **explain** the rationale for the differences between NewCo and CoreCo.

c. Aguirre **explains that** trade-offs are inevitable.

d. In fact, sports players' reliance on coaches may **explain why** so many of them make mistakes in life and lose most of their money after their athletic careers are over.

Some Vs may take either [*with* NP] or [*that* clause].

+v, [___ {*with* NP, *that*-S}]

(55) agree, argue

(56) a. We're not here to **argue with** the public.

b. In *A Whole New Mind*, Pink **argues that** what really matters is, well, meaning. And beauty. And empathy. And joyfulness. Those and other innately human qualities produce the kinds of innovations.

Some Vs may take an NP plus a PP.

+v, [___ NP PP]

(57) a. Yemen's opposition on Sunday **accused** [$_{NP}$ **outgoing President Ali Abdullah Saleh**] [$_{PP}$ **of trying to torpedo a power transfer deal by sparking a new crisis**], as troops loyal to him clashed with opposition forces, killing three.

b. Meeting with high school students at the International Studies Learning Center near Los Angeles, he joked that he wished he had more free time, "but to **borrow** [$_{NP}$ **the title**] [$_{PP}$ **from an American film**], it's like *Mission: Impossible*."

+v, [___ {NP, PP}]

Some Vs may take an NP or PP.

(58) a. By the time we **meet** [$_{NP}$ **him**], he has served a prison term and is an armed killer and brothel owner.

b. On Tuesday, Clinton is to **meet** [$_{PP}$ **with Ivory Coast President Alassane Ouattara**], who won a 2010 election but relied on his forces and international help to oust predecessor Laurent Gbagbo.

Meaning Difference

The string of [V + P] may change the meaning of a clause depending on the word choice of a P.

(59) a. But less than a year after it opened, the Texas Consumer Health Assistance Program is preparing to shut down, a victim of Congress's inability to **agree on** a federal budget for next year.

[= to decide]

b. Rubio said that clearing these obstacles and creating a realistic plan to reduce the debt and deficit would lead to greater prosperity, which would lead to more jobs, which would mean more taxpayers and therefore more revenue for, among other things, Medicare funding and infrastructure repairs. You won't find a Republican who doesn't **agree with** this assessment, but you also won't find any who can deliver the argument with greater passion or less-divisive rhetoric.

[= to have the same opinion]

(60) a. As you well know, several causes may contribute to an event or situation, and several effects may **result from** an event or situation; however, those causes and those consequences don't necessarily carry equal importance.

[= Sth is caused by another.]

b. There's the Dodd-Frank act, which will **result in** a few hundred more banking rules and force him to hire another employee.

[= to make sth happen]

(61) a. He doesn't **conform to** the stereotype of a military man.

[= be similar to sth]

b. We **conformed with** social and family expectations.

[= to obey sth]

Exercise 9

9_1

Choose the best prepositions to complete the following sentences:

(62) Governments and corporations find they're coming (above, below, over, under) attack by a new and dangerous enemy.

(63) How much of an impact does so-called gay money have (at, for, in, on) gay rights?

(64) Former President Clinton compares the chaos in Syria (to, with) Rwanda and whether the U.S. should intervene now.

(65) Amazon's Kindle Fire is a solid tablet, and a relative bargain (at, in, on) $199. But Apple's iPad is still ahead (at, of, on, with) the field.

(66) Three people died (after, at, during, in, with) clashes (after, at, during, in, with) police (after, at, during, in, with) Jos, hours (after, at, during, in, with) a car bomb killed five people (after, at, during, in, with) services (after, at, during, in, with) a church.

(67) Neil Curry reports (at, of, on, over) the popularity (at, of, on, over) comic book super heroes (at, of, on, over) the big screen (at, of, on, over) the years.

(68) Becky Anderson looks (at, from, in, of, to) tweets (at, from, in, of, to) celebrities (at, from, in, of, to) reaction (at, from, in, of, to) President Obama's support (at, from, in, of, to) gay marriage.

(69) New details continue (about, by, to) emerge (about, by, to) the agent sent (about, by, to) Saudi intelligence officials (about, by, to) infiltrate al Qaeda.

(70) Marketplace Europe looks (at, during, of) how the Parisian pawn industry is booming (at, during, of) a time (at, during, of) austerity.

(71) A father leaps (after, at, of, to) his daughter's rescue (after, at, of, to) she unlocks the car door and tumbles out (after, at, of, to) the moving vehicle.

(72) Rebekah Brooks testifies (at, into, over, to) links (at, into, over, to) politicians (at, into, over, to) a UK government-backed inquiry (at, into, over, to) phone hacking and press ethics.

(73) Louie Cordero has been conjuring (for, in, over, up) canvasses and sculptures (for, in, over, up) his Manila studio (for, in, over, up) ten years.

(74) The Dalai Lama refused (about, in, of, to) answer a question (about, in, of, to) monk self-immolations (about, in, of, to) protest (about, in, of, to) China's occupation (about, in, of, to) Tibet.

9_2

Underline every PP in each sentence, and specify its grammatical function as A or Adv:

[e.g.] Many industries <u>from the US</u> (A) have built manufacturing plants <u>in Mexico</u> (Adv) <u>in recent years</u> (Adv).

(75) The migration of birds is a fascinating subject.

(76) On Tuesday mornings the students from my study group take walking tours.

(77) During the night our dog cornered a skunk behind the garage.

(78) Quiz shows on television became popular again with many viewers.

Busy Prepositions

[Words and Music by Bob Dorough]

Like a butterfly or like a bee
Like an ant as busy as can be
These little words we call the Busy "Ps"
Prepositions!

Nine or ten of them do most all of the work
Of, on, to, with, in, from, by, for, at, over, across
And many others do their jobs
Which is simply to connect
Their noun or pronoun object to some other word in the sentence.
Busy P's if you please

On the top is where you are
(On the top relates to where)
With a friend you'll travel far
(With a friend you'll go)
If you try you know that you can fly
Over the rainbow
(Over the rainbow is where you can fly)

Busy prepositions
Always on the go
Like a bunch of busy bees
Floating pollen on the breeze
Buzzing over the meadows
Beyond the forest, through the trees, into the beehive

10 Multiword Verbs

There are two types of multiword Vs: phrasal Vs and prepositional Vs. They should be differentiated from each other. For example, *looked* is a phrasal V in (1a) but a prepositional V in (1b).

(1) a. John [$_{V}$ **looked up**] the word in a dictionary. [= to try to find information]

b. John **looked** [$_{PP}$ **up** the sky].

10.1 Phrasal Verbs

Phrasal Vs behave as one single V, consisting of a V and a particle. There are seven patterns as follows:

+v, [___ Particle]

In this pattern, phrasal Vs are used only intransitively.

(2) break out, catch on, check up, come in, crop up, get by, give in, go away, grow up, look in, ring off, start out, stay up, stop off, take off, wait up, watch out, wear off

(3) a. Rain drummed on the roofs of the Scout and the Willys. On the slickers of the two dead men. It was the only sound until the crow **took off** from the telephone wire with a raucous caw. [= to fly]

b. Still, from time to time, and in consequence of this very movement, the ancient slang **crops up** again and becomes new once more. [= to happen or appear unexpectedly]

c. When World War I **breaks out**, Albert's dad sells Joey to the army. The film follows Joey's experiences on the battlefield. [= to start]

+v, [___ Particle NP]

In this pattern, phrasal Vs are transitive and inseparable.

(4) fall for, feel for, grow on, look after, part with, pick on, run across, set about, take after

(5) He wouldn't be sentenced until the summer, but the weeks since he had gotten out of jail had been dispiriting. He was trying to {**look after** his daughter, *__look__ his daughter **after**}, but job interviews kept stalling when his record came up. [= to take care of sb or sth]

(6) I went poking along over rough ground for a quarter of a mile or more, and then {**run across** a big old-fashioned double loghouse, *__run__ a big old-fashioned double loghouse **across**}. [= to meet sb or find sth unexpectedly]

In this pattern, phrasal Vs are transitive but should be separated by the complement.

+v, [___ NP Particle]

(7) answer back, ask in, call back, catch out, count in, get down, get off, invite out, order about, tell apart

(8) 'Girls, girls, do be quiet one minute! I must {get this off, *get off this} by the early mail, and you drive me distracted with your worry,' cried Mrs. March, crossing out the third spoiled sentence in her letter. [= to send a letter or parcel to sb]

(9) The instructor's attitude is {getting the class down, *getting down the class}. [= to make sb unhappy]

(10) But above all Denisov must not dare to imagine that I'll obey him and that he can {order me about, *order about me}. I will certainly go to the French camp with Dolokhov. If he can, so can I! [= to tell sb what they should do]

(11) Quincey held out his hand. "{Count me in, *Count in me}," he said. "You and the Dutchman will tell me what to do, and I'll do it." [= to include sb in an activity]

In this pattern, phrasal Vs are transitive and can be separated by the complement. Note, however, that when the complement is a weak ProN as in (13b), it should appear between the phrasal V and its particle. In this case, the weak ProN functions as a sort of clitics in French and should be incorporated into the V phonologically.

+v, [{ ___ Particle NP, ___ NP Particle}]

(12) add on, bring up, call up, fold up, hand over, knock over, point out, pull down, put away, put up, rub out, sort out, take up, tear up, throw away, try out, turn up

(13) a. In Vladivostok, the Red Cross {put up the children, put the children up} in a former barracks on nearby Russky Island, now under feverish development for the Asian-Pacific Economic Cooperation summit in September. [= to let sb stay]

b. The Red Cross {*put up it, put it up} in a former barracks.

(14) On the day of her keynote, the hotel halls were slightly emptier, and workers were starting to {fold up tables, fold tables up}. [= to make sth into a smaller and neater shape by folding it]

(15) If a fire alarm sounds and if you have time, {turn off all gas and electric appliances, turn all gas and electric appliances off} before leaving the building. [= to switch off]

+v, [___ Particle (NP)]

In this pattern, phrasal Vs can be used both transitively and intransitively.

(16) a. In the perpetual struggle of selfish interests, his heart grew cold, then contracted, and then dried up. [= to stop being available]

b. Only some thirsty arid summers had he seen; those summers had dried up all his physical superfluousness. But this, his thinness, so to speak, seemed no more the token of wasting anxieties and cares, than it seemed the indication of any bodily blight. [= to end sth]

+v, [___ Particle PP]

In this pattern, phrasal Vs consist of a V followed by a particle and a P.

(17) break out of, catch up with, come up with, get on with, go down with, keep on at, look up to, make off with, miss out on, play around with, put up with, run away with, stick up for, talk down to, walk out on

(18) a. That in itself has been really a blessing and an honor to be able to share my story and to have other young girls **look up** [$_{PP}$ **to** me]. [= to respect sb]

b. But does Apple's surge to pre-eminence, along with the imminent flotation of Facebook, a social-networking giant, indicate that the stock market is back to the insane days of the late 1990s? There are certainly warning signs. Brokers are competing to **come up** [$_{PP}$ **with** the highest potential price target] for Apple's shares, and the announcement of a share buy-back should remind investors that companies have a tendency to purchase their own equity at market peaks. [= to think of sth]

c. The police will **catch up** [$_{PP}$ **with** you] sooner or later. [= to arrest sb who has committed a crime]

d. But there also were women whose shrewdness, self-discipline or training helped them get more of what they needed from their families. Other women simply **put up** [$_{PP}$ **with** modern life's messes]. Still others happily took on most family-related tasks. I admired these women, wished I was one of them. [= to tolerate or accept sb or sth]

In this pattern, phrasal Vs consist of a V, a complement, and a particle followed by a PP.

+v, [___ NP Particle PP]

(19) do sth out of, let sth in for, put sth down to, put sth up to, take sb up on, talk sb out of

(20) a. I've decided to **take** you **up** [**on** that job offer].
[= to accept an offer or invitation]

b. His father **talked** him **out** [**of** moving out].
[= to persuade sb not to do sth]

10.2 Prepositional Verbs

+v, [___ PP]

Prepositional Vs are composed of a V followed by a P with which it is closely associated.

(21) a. I stared [$_{PP}$ at the sky] as directed.

b. "The more I investigated," Hope said, "the more I realized that most public schools allow this, so it troubled me that some schools decided [$_{PP}$ on their own] and that they didn't think this was very important."

Prepositional Vs do not take the P-movement rule.

(22) a. *I stared ___ the sky at as directed.

b. *It troubled me that some schools decided ___ their own on and that they didn't think this was very important.

The V and the following P can be separated by an Adv.

(23) We're going to decide mainly [$_{PP}$ on integrity and morality].

The P can precede a wh-relative ProN or a wh-interrogative ProN.

(24) a. With his consummate knowledge of the nature of the people with whom he had to deal, he anticipated every measure on which they decided ___.

b. On what is Ted deciding ___?

The shaded strings below apparently look like prepositional Vs, but they should be distinguished: [V NP A] or [*be* A P].

+v, [___ NP A],
+v, [___ A P]

(25) a. "Don't be so impatient," said Snow White. "I will try to think." She clapped her hands as if she had discovered a remedy, took out her scissors, and in a moment **set the dwarf free** by cutting off the end of his beard.

b. I suggest you continue to be in occasional contact with these people because you **are fond of** them, and they are obviously fond of you.

Exercise 10

10_1

Select the particle or preposition that best completes each sentence:

(26) She spends her evenings poring (at, for, over, with) textbooks.

(27) The Obama campaign pulled (in, off, on, out) the biggest fundraiser in presidential history.

(28) It is the mechanical element that usually crops (at, down, on, up) in any story.

10_2

Analyze each sentence as represented in the example, and specify whether multiword verbs are phrasal or prepositional:

[e.g.] Mary looked up the word.

[Answer: *Mary / looked up / the word. Phrasal V*]

(29) Mary looked up the hill.

(30) The police are looking into the suspect's activities.

(31) The office closes down on the weekends.

(32) Mary stood by the door.

(33) The defense wrapped up its case.

(34) The judge threw out the verdict.

11 Transitivity

11.1 Verbal System

Vs can be classified as in (1). There are two kinds of Vs in English: Aux Vs and non-Aux Vs. Aux Vs are helping Vs, which are composed of modals, aspectual auxiliaries, passive auxiliaries, dummy auxiliaries, and emphatic auxiliaries. In modals, you have primary modals such as *will* or *would*, and secondary modals such as *have to* or *ought to*. There are only two kinds of aspectual auxiliaries in English: *have* and *be*. *Have* is the perfect Aux, and *be* the progressive Aux. *Be* is used as the passive Aux, too. *Do* is the dummy Aux in negative and interrogative clauses. *Do* can be used as an emphatic Aux in positive sentences and *be* imperatives. Main Vs and linking Vs are non-Aux. According to transitivity, there are two kinds of main Vs: transitives and intransitives. According to the number of internal arguments, transitives are further classified as monotransitives, ditransitives, and complex transitives. Monotransitives like *love* take one internal argument. Ditransitives like *give* take two internal arguments. Complex transitives like *consider* take one internal argument (i.e., object) and one object complement. Intransitives are mono-argumental Vs. According to the thematic role of the external argument (i.e., subject), intransitives are further classified as ergatives (= unaccusatives) and unergatives. Ergatives like *arrive* assign a theme thematic role to the subject. Unergatives like *run* assign an agent thematic role to the subject. Linking Vs link a subject with a subject complement. A typical instance of linking Vs is copular *be*. Sensory Vs like *smell* or *taste* and non-sensory V like *appear* or *seem* belong to linking Vs, too.

Verbal System

(1)					
	Aux	Modal	Primary		*will, would*
			Secondary		*have to, ought to*
		Non-Modal	Aspectual		*be, have*
			Passive		*be*
			Dummy		*do*
			Emphatic		*do*
	Non-Aux	Main	Transitive	Monotransitive	*love*
				Ditransitive	*give*
				Complex Transitive	*consider*
			Intransitive	Ergative	*arrive*
				Unergative	*run*
		Linking	Copula		*be*
			Sensory		*smell, taste*
			Non-Sensory		*appear, seem*

The following Vs are polysemous. They have more than one meaning.

Polysemy

(2) call, fit, lose, manage, miss, move, play, run, show, spread

(3) a. We will **miss** and cherish her forever. [= to feel sad]

b. The winner will capture the division title and host a first-round NFC playoff game next weekend. The loser will **miss** the playoffs. [= to fail to experience sth]

c. I **missed** the mark with the ball. [= to fail to hit sth]

d. He didn't **miss** his wallet until the waiter brought the bill. [= to notice that sth is lost]

11.2 Intransitive Verbs

Intransitive Vs are used without an object.

(4) The politician died suddenly.

Intransitive Vs are not used in the passive.

(5) If you {**wait**, ***are waited**} for the exchange rate and interest rates to be fully liberalized, he says, you may {**wait**, ***be waited**} forever.

Unergative Vs are monoargumental. They appear with the subject argument which usually plays the role of an agent as in (6a). They normally do not choose an object as in (6b). But some of them may tolerate a cognate object (i.e., an N of the same semantic origin) especially when they are modified as in (7). Some of unergative Vs are illustrated in (8).

Unergative

(6) a. Serena laughed.

b. *Serena laughed Dan.

(7) a. to dance a tribal dance

b. to die a beautiful death

c. to sleep a troubled sleep

d. to sing a mellow song

(8) bark, chew, dance, die, dream, jump, laugh, live, run, shout, sing, sleep, talk, walk

Ergative

Ergative Vs are unaccusative Vs. The surface subject of ergative V constructions semantically plays the role of a verbal object.

(9) a. begin, break, change, crack, dry, end, freeze, grow, improve, increase, slow, start

b. bake, boil, cook, defrost, fry, melt, roast, simmer

c. balance, close, drop, move, open, rest, rock, shake, stand, turn

d. back, drive, reverse, sail, crash, fly, run

(10) a. The milk **froze**. [Ergative = Unaccusative]

b. They **froze** the milk. [Transitive]

(11) Time **froze** and a supernatural being who looked just like a human being pulled me aside and told me that I had a choice between being blinded but loved by my father and retaining my vision.

(12) While the meat **is cooking**, prepare the roll. Butter the bottom half very lightly. Spread the top half with mayonnaise.

(13) Open and closed containers of beer were found in the sport-utility vehicle that **crashed** into a fence and tree [at] about 3 a.m. [on] New Year's Day in Bethesda, killing two people and injuring three others, all of them between the ages of 18 and 22.

Middle

On the other hand, a set of *ergative* Vs has often been called *middle* Vs, as illustrated in (14). Middle Vs differ from ergative Vs in that they strongly require an adverbial or the negation *not* as in (15).

(14) anger, break, bribe, clean, drive, read, scare, sell, start, tease

(15) a. Porcelain **breaks easily**.

b. This book is a page-turner; it really **reads well**.

c. The car **starts quickly**.

d. The new model did **not sell**.

11.3 Transitive Verbs

Monotransitive

Transitive Vs are used with an object. The following transitive Vs take only one object. In this light, they are called *monotransitive* (= single-transitive) Vs.

(16) a. John **loves** Mary (*Susan).

b. If analysis **shows** that someone's brilliant work fails again and again as soon as cooperation from others is required, it probably **indicates** a lack of courtesy (*a lack of manners).

Transitive Vs are used in the passive.

(17) a. Your arrangement of beautiful food will not make much of a final impression if you **forget** this rule.

b. Your arrangement of beautiful food will not make much of a final impression if this rule **is forgotten** (by you).

Ditransitive

Ditransitive Vs (= double-transitive Vs) require a direct object (DO) and an indirect object (IO).

(18) Call your coaches and be proactive. Ask them to **send** [$_{NP}$ you] [$_{NP}$ a copy of the team's summer workout packets] so you can start to prepare.

+v, [___ NP NP]

In the following ditransitive constructions, the IO is either a ProN or a short NP.

(19) a. Challenging the government in a time of war is a terrifying thing. When I did it a few years ago on behalf of Guantanamo detainees, I took comfort from Gordon's actions. It isn't easy to be attacked as disloyal, but his life **gave** [$_{NP}$ me] strength.

b. But each insists he is well positioned to rally divided conservative voters around him and stop the advance of Romney, whose back-to-back wins in Iowa and New Hampshire have **lent** [$_{NP}$ his campaign] an air of inevitability.

+v, [___ NP *for* NP]

In the following ditransitive constructions, the IO is realized as a [*for* NP].

(20) book, buy, cook, cut, find, keep, make, paint, pour, prepare, save, win

(21) a. He saved some of his strongest comments [PP for discussing Syria].

b. While all around them newlyweds revel in newfound bliss and older couples celebrate anniversaries, Art and Marion have booked a top-floor bridal suite [PP for the final weekend of their marriage].

In the following ditransitive constructions, the IO is realized as a [*to* NP].

+v, [___ NP *to* NP]

(22) give, hand, lend, offer, pass, pay, post, promise, read, sell, send, show, teach, tell

(23) a. When the 84-year-old agreed to drive her to the Bank of America branch down the street, the suspect handed the kids [PP to another woman], police said.

b. After retiring in 2005, Mr. Gilbert concentrated on photography and international travel. He often sold his photographs [PP to commercial stock agencies].

Some Vs permit the [NP NP] pattern only.

+v, [___ NP NP] only

(24) allow, beg, forgive, spare

(25) He must hope that Republican voters will forgive {him his excesses, *his excesses for him} and look to the other side of the ledger.

Some Vs permit the [NP PP] pattern only.

+v, [___ NP PP] only

(26) admit, contribute, describe, explain, return, pronounce

(27) a. We need more people to come to this country, ready to work and to contribute {their creativity to our economy, *our economy their creativity}.

b. At his trial, which began April 16, he pronounced {the maximum penalty for his actions, *his actions the maximum penalty}—21 years in prison, or longer.

c. The manager of the Dallas and Fort Worth reps described {the techniques to other managers, *other managers the techniques} during a conference call.

Complex Transitive

The following illustrates a case of complex transitive Vs. Below, the verb *consider* is a complex transitive in that it selects an NP object followed by an object complement such as {NP, AP, PP}.

(28) a. We consider [$_{NP}$ them] [$_{NP}$ our rivals].

b. He might consider [$_{NP}$ Tuesday's results] [$_{AP}$ genuinely super].

c. We want you to consider [$_{NP}$ this] [$_{PP}$ as the people's building].

11.4 Object-deleting Verbs

Most English transitive verbs cannot permit object omission even when linguistic or situational contexts clearly indicate what the understood object is.

(29) a. *I'll open an account if you open ∅. (Quirk et al. 1985)

b. *Please give me a book to read if you have ∅.

c. *Bill liked Mary, and John liked ∅ too.

d. *What happened to that carrot? I chopped ∅.

(30) [When it is perfectly clear to the addressee that a particular door is in question]
*Did you **lock** ∅? (Fillmore 1986)

Some verbs, interestingly, may permit object omission.

(31) a. Mary **ate** ∅.

b. John is sick. I **know** ∅.

c. [On the instruction label of a medicine bottle] **Shake** ∅ well before use.

d. The number of cars in Beijing has more than doubled within the past decade, with only an estimated 740,000 spaces in which to **park** ∅. A year ago the city took an obvious step, mandating an overnight fourfold increase in parking fees.

e. Maher Ali, 17, said the Islamists amputated his hand after he robbed a store. He said he **stole** ∅ because he was unemployed and hungry.

11.5 Cognate Verbs

Cognate Vs are normally intransitive, but can be used with an object that is closely related to the V.

(32) dance (a dance), die (a death), dream (a dream), laugh (a laugh), live (a life), sigh (a sigh), smile (a smile)

(33) a. He hopes his body can be an example of a human being who **died** a natural **death**, a death without extended suffering.

b. Emma began to **laugh** a strident, piercing, continuous **laugh**; she had an attack of hysterics.

c. That may not be an event to you, but I **live** a very drab **life**, so I'm all hyped.

d. Irons **smiled** his beautiful, ironic **smile** and fluttered his gorgeously long, thin, expressive hands as he explained that, back in the late 15th/early 16th century, the pope was more of a monarch than a pope.

11.6 Reflexive Verbs

Most of transitive Vs can be used with a reflexive ProN. In this case, they are called reflexive Vs.

(34) amuse, blame, cut, dry, help, hurt, introduce, kill, prepare, repeat, restrict, satisfy, teach

(35) The scene was reminiscent of T.J. Houshmandzadeh's mea culpa after he dropped a pass that would have given the team a first down on fourth and 18 in last year's 31-24 loss to the Pittsburgh Steelers in the AFC divisional round. Much like Evans, Houshmandzadeh **blamed himself** for not making a play when one was needed.

Some Vs as in (36) do not normally select reflexive ProNs. Exceptionally, however, reflexive ProNs are used with these Vs for emphasis.

(36) dress (up), shave, wash

(37) a. They **dressed up** for a fancy dinner.

b. Whatever Tess's reasoning, some spirit had induced her to **dress herself up** neatly as she had formerly done, and come out into the fields, harvest-hands being greatly in demand just then. [= to put on formal clothes for a special occasion]

On the whole, *behave* does not select an object. When it selects an object, however, the object must be a reflexive ProN.

(38) a. The importance of a professional attitude begins even before you start your first job. The standard advice for a successful job interview applies to cooks as well as to office professionals: Dress and behave not for the group you belong to but for the group you want to join. Arrive neat, clean, appropriately dressed, and on time. Get noticed for the right reasons. Carry this attitude through every day on the job.

b. One afternoon he had been sent out with them a long time, and when James brought him in and put on his halter, he said: "There, you rogue, mind how you behave {yourself, *you, *him}, or we shall get into trouble."

Some Vs as in (39) mainly select an impersonal object, but not a personal object. When they select a personal object, however, the object must be a reflexive ProN.

(39) apply, compose, distance, enjoy, excel, exert, express, strain

(40) a. Could you express your limiting principle as succinctly as you possibly can?

b. A musician should make sure his basic principles are right, then express {himself, *him} according to his temperament.

The following Vs are true reflexives in that they select only a reflexive object.

+v, [___ reflexive ProN]

(41) a. Shower upon him every earthly blessing, drown him in a sea of happiness, so that nothing but bubbles of bliss can be seen on the surface; give him economic prosperity, such that he should

have nothing else to do but sleep, eat cakes and busy {himself, *him} with the continuation of his species.

b. A generous buffet will magically appear in the hall outside, but for now Jolie must content {herself, *her} with a small bottle of water that she idly seesaws up and down while talking about her new movie.

11.7 Reciprocal Verbs

Reciprocal Vs show a two-way relationship. They suggest that two entities are doing the same thing to each other. For emphasis, they accompany reflexive ProNs: *each other* or *one another*.

(42) argue, clash, coincide, combine, compete, cuddle, divorce, fight, hug, kiss, marry, match, meet, separate, touch

(43) a. It is difficult to imagine Alain de Botton and Roger Scruton becoming friends if they met at a party.

b. Before arriving in Delhi, Mr. Hu met Barack Obama, America's president, for 90 minutes on the sidelines of a nuclear-security summit in Seoul.

c. We have only met each other once before, you know.

Some reciprocal Vs are sensitive to specific Ps.

(44) a. They don't fight with each other with courage that's born in them, but with courage that's borrowed from their mass.

b. In the aftermath of the unexpected early death of Alexander the Great, his friends and family fought against each other for supremacy and control over the vast new Hellenistic Empire.

(45) a. We parted with each other with great heartiness on both sides.

b. Ted and Robin parted from each other for their sake.

(46) a. They hugged and talked with each other.

b. But there's been little progress getting computer systems to talk to one another to exchange data the way financial companies do.

11.8 Light Verbs

The following common Vs are light Vs in that they have very little meaning. The major meaning of the predicate is located on the verbal N.

(47) do, give, go, have, make, take

(48) a. I laid there, and had a good rest and a smoke out of my pipe, looking away into the sky; not a cloud in it.

b. He made his first visit to Verizon Center.

c. I have had similar experiences with an anesthesiologist who was reluctant to sedate me fully before a surgical procedure and an OB/GYN who gave me poor advice about insulin use.

d. A convalescing patient who does not finish the full course of treatment takes a grave risk.

e. At Silk Street Market, a digital banner welcomes the delegates to town and invites them to go shopping.

f. Hire a qualified, licensed exterminator who knows how to use poisons, insecticides, and traps. Most poisons should not be used in a food production operation, so it's better not to do the job yourself.

11.9 Information Principles

Two information-structuring principles help determine the choice of pattern in sentences with an indirect object: the Given-New Contract and the End-Weight Principle.

Given-New

According to the Given-New Contract, new information should be linked to something that is given. It is highly likely that listeners or readers understand more easily if each utterance or statement starts with what is familiar and proceeds onto what is new.

+v, [___ NP_{IO} NP_{DO}]

For instance, if an IO is given information in a ditransitive construction, the [NP NP] pattern is preferred.

(49) And there is a faint possibility that it will lead to much more than that. **Kim Jong Un** appears to want stable foreign relations as **he** consolidates power. But if **he** really does end up taking a different path from **his** father, then **he** will need vast amounts of foreign support. America is right to {give **him** the chance, ?give the chance to **him**}. The six-party talks on the nuclear program could yet be the forum in which the outside world invests in North Korean power stations and infrastructure.

+v, [___ NP_{DO} PP_{IO}]

If a DO is given information, the [NP PP] pattern is preferred.

(50) Gates and Buffett follow Andrew Carnegie's admonition to the rich to avoid the flashy high life. The "duty of the man of wealth," Carnegie said in 1889, is "to set an example of modest, unostentatious living, shunning display or extravagance; to provide modestly for the legitimate wants of those dependent upon him; and, after doing so,"

to use the rest of their money for "the most beneficial results for the community." Yet even as Americans admire those who give it away, a consistent majority of the public remains suspicious of estate taxes, believing that if you make a lot of money, you ought to be able to {give money to your children, ?give your children money}. "There's a double standard in our psyche that hasn't changed through our history," says Arizona State University law professor Marjorie Kornhauser, who has written about how U.S. tax policies reflect our confusion over the morality of money. "We have very mixed attitudes toward the rich."

End-Weight

According to the End-Weight Principle, a long and complex NP can be moved to the sentence-final position in order to enhance clarity and facilitate understanding.

(51) You can look at what a lot of people consider one of the greatest speeches, the Gettysburg Address. Edward Everett, who spoke before Lincoln that day, {??gave a speech that was two-hours long to the audience, gave the audience a speech that was two-hours long}. Lincoln's lasted three minutes.

(52) The panelists discuss with host Melissa Harris-Perry the political ramifications of President Obama's announcement that he supports same-sex marriage.

Exercise 11

11_1

Select the word that best completes each sentence:

(53) A convenience store owner fought back (against, with) bear spray and a spanking when he was confronted by two would-be thieves.

(54) Sidner (commits, does, makes, takes) a closer look at the fight to improve working conditions in Bangladesh.

(55) Apple CEO Tim Cook (does, goes, has, makes) a rare public appearance at the All Things D technology conference. Simon reports.

(56) Rachman discusses (that, what, whether, which) a federal Europe could solve the financial crisis.

(57) Wyatt tracks (how, that, what, which) the online community has responded (to, for, at, with) racism comments made by FIFA president Sepp Blatter.

11_2

Select the verb that best completes each sentence:

(58) The name of all the continents (ends, end) with the same letter that they start with.

(59) In 1659, Massachusetts (makes, made) Christmas illegal.

(60) However, on the edge of the art world, new types of art (exists, exist).

(61) Finding exhibits of computer graphics in an art exhibit (comes, come) as a surprise to more traditional museum visitors.

(62) In these new courses, the literary aspect of computer games, as well as their graphics, (is, are) studied.

(63) Either the coach or her assistant (decides, decide) where the games should be played.

(64) Neither the teacher nor the students (was, were) consulted about the test results.

(65) Two weeks of winter vacation (is, are) not enough time to truly relax.

(66) (Do, Does) either of the dancers perform regularly?

(67) Most of meat (was, were) imported from Argentina.

(68) (Is, Are) physics a required course for engineering school?

(69) Beyond the meadow and near the river (is, are) some lovely campgrounds.

(70) Hours of driving (lay, laid) ahead of us.

(71) Our applications were (lying, laying) in front of the file.

(72) Last night's victory really (rose, raised) the team's spirit and confidence.

(73) Tempers (rose, raised) as the debate progressed.

11_3

Underline every verb group in the following sentences:

[e.g.] Have you seen the baby mammoth in the display?

She looked the word up in the dictionary.

(74) She would have been delighted to see you.

(75) All of the displays feature artifacts still used by local tribes.

(76) The boys had been looking for a secret passage to the Castle.

(77) The boys do not guess the ages of the paintings.

11_4

Put the words in parentheses in the right order to make sentences:

(78) Recent box office hits show that good acting and a good storyline (more, special effects, contribute, than, to a film's success).

(79) We look at some helpful ways for parents to make (fun, holiday, this, safe, and, scary) for their kids.

12 Tenses

When Grammar Meets Linguistics

Time vs. Tense

Time is physical, whereas *tense* is grammatical. How many time relations can you imagine? 12?

(1) {present, past, future} x {simple, progressive, perfect, perfect progressive} = 12

Maybe. How many tenses are there in English grammar? 12? No. There is no reason to assume that there should be one-to-one correspondence between physical time and grammatical time.

(2) Time: Tense $\neq$ 1: 1

Tense expresses time. It refers to the moment of utterance. Morphologically, English marks only present and past time by inflections on Vs. In this light, it has been often claimed in linguistics that English has only two tenses: present tense and past tense. It was thus claimed that the other time relations are expressed in a different manner. For the sake of convenience, however, we use the conventional way of describing the notions of time vs. tense.

12.1 Auxiliary Verbs

Aux Vs are helping Vs. *Be, have*, and *do* are (non-modal) auxiliaries (Auxes). They take VPs as their complements.

(3) a. The recipes in this book are planned and organized to reinforce the basic skills the student **is** [$_{VP}$ learning].

b. While the publisher and author **have** [$_{VP}$ used their best efforts in preparing this book], they make no representations or warranties with respect to the accuracy or completeness of the contents of this book and specifically disclaim any implied warranties of merchantability or fitness for a particular purpose.

c. You are sauteing beef tenderloin tips for stroganoff, and you suddenly find that the meat is simmering in liquid rather than sauteing. What **did** you [$_{VP}$ do wrong]?

Aspect

Aspect is a grammatical term which encodes the length of time an action, event, or situation has gone on.[♣] There are two kinds of aspect in English: progressive and perfect. These two aspects in English may combine in a complex VP.

♣ According to Greenbaum and Quirk (1990: 51), aspect reflects the way in which the action of a verb is viewed with respect to time. According to DeCarrico (2000: 198), aspect is a grammatical category of a verb that encodes the internal time structure of the action, event, or situation. According to Huddleston and Pullum (2005: 295), aspect indicates the speaker's view of the temporal structure of the situation the clause describes, such as whether it is habitual or complete.

(4) a. present perfect, past perfect

b. present progressive, past progressive

c. present perfect progressive, past perfect progressive

Aux *be* is used in progressive tenses.

be

(5) The growth of the food service industry creates a demand for thousands of skilled people every year. Many people are attracted by a career that **is** challeng**ing** and excit**ing** and, above all, provides the chance to find real satisfaction in doing a job well.

Aux *be* is used in passive sentences.

(6) Much kitchen terminology **is** tak**en** from French. Phonetic guides **are** includ**ed** for difficult words, giving the approximate pronunciation using English sounds. Exact rendering is impossible in many cases, because French has a number of sounds that don't exist in English.

Aux *have* is used in perfect tenses.

have

(7) Rather, they are based on an understanding of how different foods react when heated in various ways, when combined in various proportions, and so on. The chefs who **have** **come** before us **have** already **done** much of this work so we don't have to.

Dummy *do* is used in negative or question sentences.

do

(8) a. In a healthy economy, entrepreneurs with ideas can easily start companies, the best of which grow fast and the worst of which are quickly swept aside. Size **doesn't** matter. Growth does.

b. Are you looking for challenging work? Do you want to contribute to Latin America and the Caribbean?

The shaded *do* in the following is a main V.

(9) "It was partly to get you to do something," I conceded. "But, you know, you didn't do it."

Emphatic *do* is used in both positive and imperative sentences.

(10) a. These limitations don't invalidate standardized recipes. If anything, they make exact directions even more important. But they do mean that experience and knowledge are still very important.

b. 'Girls, girls, do be quiet one minute! I must get this off by the early mail, and you drive me distracted with your worry,' cried Mrs. March, crossing out the third spoiled sentence in her letter.

c. I know, dear, I know. But do [try and be realistic about it].

Ordering

You may have several Aux Vs. In this case, the order given in (11) should be observed. In order to derive (12), an affix such as *-en* or *-ing* hops onto the following verbal stem.

(11)	a.	[Modal	Perfect	Progressive	Passive]	Main V
	b.	[Modal	*have-en*	*be-ing*	*be-en*]	Main V

(12) a. The book must have been being written.

b. Betsy must have been being hassled by the police.

12.2 Present Tense

The present tenses cover *present simple*, *present progressive*, *present perfect*, and *present perfect progressive* time.

(13) a. I work.

b. I am working.

c. I have worked.

d. I have been working.

Present Simple

The present simple tense refers to general present things.

(14) a. At heart he's a genuine, simple guy who loves the Lord, loves his family and loves to compete in football.

b. Mr. & Mrs. Lanphere reside in Arlington, Virginia.

The present simple tense refers to a regular or habitual action.

(15) a. Some big British firms minimize their tax bills so aggressively that they provoke outrage. Films nearly always depict big business as malign.

b. "I think when you play quarterback in the National Football League, you have to understand that you are going to have bumps and bruises throughout the way," Romo said during a conference call with reporters.

The present simple tense refers to general truths.

(16) a. Water **boils** at 212 degrees Fahrenheit, so use that as a test.

b. Hot water can be poured over the small pot; when the moisture **evaporates**, the tea is ready.

The present simple tense indicates a statement about fixed dates.

(17) "Oh, yes! I know that! I know that, but do you know what day it is?" On my saying that I did not understand, she went on: "It **is** the eve of St. George's Day. Do you not know that tonight, when the clock strikes midnight, all the evil things in the world will have full sway?"

Present Progressive

The present progressive tense refers to a temporary situation.

(18) a. University students in Khartoum **are rallying** against budget cuts and **demanding** Omar al-Bashir's ouster.

b. As volunteer Ellie Wigodsky peels apples with Banneker seniors Crawford and Sydney Porter, the talk veers from the colleges they'd like to attend to how hard it **is watching** a grandparent deal with Alzheimer's.

The present progressive may refer to future time, accompanying time adverbials.

(19) a. Everything has been total mayhem ever since, with the everyday business of the day's news utterly forgotten and everyone gibbering down the phone about links, towers and OBs. Anyway, it **is** all **happening tomorrow** and I have to report to Lewisham fire station at 11 o'clock. I'm going to ring round everybody tonight and tell them to watch.

b. His approval rating was lower in Nevada than in Virginia and North Carolina—two other states that flipped from Republican to Democrat in 2008 and that Republicans **are eyeing** to win back **next fall**.

Present Perfect (Progressive)

The present perfect tense refers to something that happened at an indefinite time in the past and is finished, but which still affects the current situation.

(20) a. Rice seems to **have forgotten** that readers don't want werewolves with good taste; they want werewolves who think humans taste good.

b. A video uploaded to the Internet by a terminally ill 17-year-old **has been watched** by more than a million people around the world. [result usage]

The present perfect tense refers to very recent things. In this usage, the present perfect tense usually accompanies an Adv such as *just*, *already*, or *yet*.

(21) a. Julie Koo, the executive director of the Mayor's Office on Asian and Pacific Islander Affairs, is also here; she **has** just **been ushered** into her seat by Tony Cheng, the eponymous restaurant owner who gallantly tells everyone at the table to order whatever they want.

b. The U.S. government **has** already **launched** a new website and is pouring millions of dollars into two large studies examining whether or not a drug can slow the progression of Alzheimer's among patients who are predisposed to the devastating disease.

c. He would turn over the reins of power to his dynamic running mate, whom he **has vowed** not to identify yet. [completeness usage]

The present perfect tense indicates that something started to happen at an indefinite time in the past and has continued to happen up to now.

(22) a. San Francisco is, in my opinion, the team of the year. This team **has had** talent for a few years but just never has been able to pull it all together.

b. You **have watched** her too long under your eyelids. [progressiveness usage]

The present perfect tense refers to something that happened at an indefinite time in the past, but it is not necessary to say when it happened.

(23) a. We threw everything away and started over again. Since then we **have been** to England and Europe well over 20 times to bring back stock.

b. I **have heard** the story many times. [experience usage]

The present perfect progressive tense has very similar meanings to the present perfect tense, but emphasizes the period of time during which an action has happened.

(24) a. NASA is counting down the seconds until its twin spacecraft bound for the moon make back-to-back arrivals over the New Year's weekend. The washing-machine-size probes **have been cruising** independently toward their destination since launching in September aboard the same rocket on a mission to measure lunar gravity.

b. About 6o churches, mostly Christian but also Buddhist, Jewish and Hindu congregations, rent space from New York City's Department of Education. But the city authorities **have been trying** to enforce a ban on worship in schools since 1996.

The present tense refers to future time in certain embedded clauses.

Present Tense vs. Future Time

(25) a. American officials say North Korea dropped its insistence on grains, and will allow an extensive international monitoring system to be installed [before food is delivered].

b. How conceited and self-satisfied he will be [when he gets my note]!

c. Your daughter will not die of grief [if he marries her].

d. No one exactly wants to make the trip there and back—but you will only be making the journey there! Wladek was still listening intently. 'When you reach the station, wait [until the prisoners' train arrives].'

e. Mr. Horace Moore left the station in great distress, after learning that his only course was to take the ordinary slow train [which leaves Liverpool at six o'clock].

In attributive (= defining, restrictive) relative clauses, the present simple tense refers to future time.

(26) The information [that you have tomorrow] will keep her alive.

In time clauses, the present perfect tense refers to future time.

(27) I will watch Ted and wait until he has dug his hole, until he has filled it and has gone away.

Stative Vs are usually not used in progressive tenses.

Stativity

(28) a. Voters are sick of happy talk and cheap attacks. They're ready for problem-solving, and they {know, *are knowing} it requires tough decisions.

b. Those tools {resemble, *are resembling} blades found in Europe.

Some stative Vs are used in progressive tenses in other meanings.

(29) a. We {have, *are having} a nice comfortable cushion. [= to own]

b. ESPN is having a viewing party Friday night when the Knicks take on the Lakers. [= to give]

c. And he says these colleges know more about how many kids attend basketball games and which alumni give money than how many students showed up for economics class during the week and which alumni are having a hard time meeting their career goals because of shortcomings in their education. [= to experience]

d. We were just having a look around. [= to do something]

e. When I came to the archway by the gallery and the staircase I heard the murmur and hum of conversation coming from the dining-room. They were still having dinner. The great hall was deserted. There was nobody in the gallery either. The band must be having their dinner too. [= to eat or drink sth]

12.3 Past Tense

English has four past tenses: past simple, past progressive, past perfect, and past perfect progressive.

(30) a. I worked.

b. I was working.

c. I had worked.

d. I had been working.

The past simple tense refers to general past things.

Past Simple

(31) And simply from the look in her eyes, which **grew** unconsciously brighter, Levin **knew** that she **loved** that man, **knew** it as surely as if she had told him so in words.

The past simple tense refers to regular or habitual actions in the past.

(32) a. Are Indian firms really going to take over the world? Until liberalization in 1991, the travel schedules of Indian executives often **revolved** around treks to Delhi to beg officials for access to hard currency and permission to import equipment.

b. Willie and Zach **managed** to see each other every day as well as weekends and odd evenings, and they, the twins and George would walk and play in the fields together.

The past tense sounds more polite than the present one.

(33) a. I intend to do honestly all he expects of me, so I am not deceiving him ... Why {**did**, do} you smile just **now**?

b. I {**was wondering**, wonder, am wondering} if you could help me.

The past progressive tense refers to something that continued to happen before and after an indefinite time in the past.

Past Progressive

(34) Evidence is growing that commonly used pesticides, even when employed carefully, are bad for bees. In the winter of 2006, beekeepers in America noticed something odd—lots of their hives **were dying** for no obvious reason.

The past progressive tense refers to a temporary situation.

(35) Mr. Harrison thinks the Kinect's basic principles could be used to make a technological panopticon (an area where everything is visible) that monitors people's movements and gives them what they want, wherever they want it. Someone in a shopping mall, for example, might hold up his hand and see a map appear instantly at his fingertips. This image might then be locked in place by the user sticking his thumb out. A visitor to a museum, armed with a suitable earpiece, could get the lowdown on what he **was looking** at simply by pointing at it.

The past (progressive) tense in conditional clauses refers to something that is less likely to happen.

(36) a. But then the police did something unusual: they sent the seven letters inviting them to police headquarters for a talk, promising that **if** they **came** they would not be arrested.

b. And it would have been fine, probably, **if** he **was running** for president of Friends of the National Zoo.

Past Perfect

The past perfect (= Pluperfect) tense expresses a past event completed prior to another past event of past time. Sentences with the past perfect often have a main clause and a subordinate clause introduced by *after, before, by the time (that), when*, and so on.

(37) a. The Washington Post asked the leaders of several D.C. theaters to talk about the small-theater scene, many declined because they **had** not **seen** many productions.

b. This provided a window of opportunity during which the project would cause minimal disruption. The decision to proceed **had** already **been made** by the time new president Wallace Loh was on board.

c. Besides criticizing the outcome, opponents of the bill also took issue Friday with the process, accusing House leaders of muscling the legislation through the chamber once they had secured just enough votes.

d. Tom had already washed the dishes when Lucy asked if she could help him.

Past Perfect (Progressive)

The past perfect (progressive) tense refers to a time which had started earlier in the past but was still continuing. For example, in (38a) fingering a golden ring started earlier than making a speech.

(38) a. As for Bilbo Baggins, even while he was making his speech, he had been fingering the golden ring in his pocket: his magic ring that he had kept secret for so many years.

b. Most killings happened amid personal disputes, often stemming from squabbles at nightclubs where people had been drinking, she said.

c. Murdock switched over to the Weather Channel. He had always hated politics and did not plan to vote, but he did love the United States and believed in the concept of opportunity.

The past perfect (progressive) tense in conditional clauses indicates something that could have happened in the past, but which did not actually happen.

(39) a. If the case had gone to trial and Kinney had been convicted, Fisher said, he was "confident" Kinney would have received a longer sentence.

b. General Manager Mike Rizzo was open to the idea, and if Harper had been knocking the cover off the ball, Rizzo would have been forced to make a tough decision. Instead, this one was fairly easy.

Duration The progressive tense shows duration, i.e., the length of time that something continues.

(40) a. Most killings happened amid personal disputes, often stemming from squabbles at nightclubs where people had been drinking, she said.

b. Saturday's protest—called Strategy 31 after the article of the constitution that guarantees freedom of assembly—has been going on for two years, held on the 31st of every month with that many days.

Note that you do not have to use progressive tenses for duration.

(41) a. A native of Winthrop, MA, he had resided in Alexandria, VA for over thirty years.

b. He worked as a computer analyst for NASA from 1967 to 1993 and contributed to space shuttle missions.

Usage The progressive tense refers to an action that requires an intentional physical or mental energy that is needed to do something as in (42). Note that stative verbs such as *think* are not used in the progressive tense as in (43).

(42) a. Gayle was a wonderful wife, mother, sister and grandmother; she was generous, and thoughtful, always thinking of others and their needs.

b. After Heidi had gone to bed that night, she lay awake a little while, thinking over everything the grandmother had said, especially about the joy the songs had given her.

(43) cf. We {think, *are thinking} that Ted knows the answer.

used to vs. *would*

Used to and *would* refer to something that occurred **regularly** in the past.

(44) This was unusual behavior for a messenger, who {would, used to} normally stop to eat and drink and rest his horse.

(45) So the performance continued to happen, once a week quite regularity, whenever it was not impossible. She even {used to, would} remind him of it in the morning, as something which had to be done that evening and which must not be forgotten.

Used to and *would* both refer to habitual actions and events in the past. However, with *would*, it is necessary to have an already established **past time-frame**. The past time-frame is often established by a previous occurrence of *used to* as in (46) or by time adverbial expressions as in (47).

(46) He had his things moved out from the dressing-room. We made up one of the rooms at the end of the corridor. I don't think he slept much even there. He used to sit in the armchair. There would be cigarette ash all round it in the morning. And in the daytime Frith would hear him in the library pacing up and down. Up and down, up and down.

(47) The river that bordered the estate became an extension to their playground. In spring they fished, in summer they swam, and in winter, when the river was frozen over, they would put on their wooden skates and chase each other across the ice, while Florentyna sat on the river bank anxiously warning them where the surface was thin.

Would is not used to refer to states in the past which are no longer true:

(48) a. A large photograph of an elderly man in yachting costume attracted me, hung on the wall over his desk. 'Who's this?' 'That? That's Mr. Dan Cody, old sport.' The name sounded faintly familiar. 'He's dead now. He {used to, *would} be my best friend years ago.'

b. Wollera {used to, *would} be a horse station years ago, selling horses to the Indian Army, but you can't sell horses now.

would vs. {*was, were*} *going to*

Would and *was/were going to* refer to future from a point of view in past time.

(49) a. After the war ended, I decided that I would not write to you or approach you, though Edmund had told me to do so.

b. Did you ever hear that he was going to marry, or had married, a French girl just before he was killed?

12.4 Future Tense

will

Will is used to indicate future time.

(50) I will report your statement tomorrow.

Will is used for indicating what you predict to happen in the future based on general beliefs.

(51) a. When the weather warms in the spring, SHA will begin milling and paving operations in this area.

b. I give you this warning, although I feel sure that he will make a favorable impression upon you.

Will refers to a decision you are about to make.

(52) Ring up and make an appointment. I {will, am about to} leave instructions with my secretary.

Will is used for indicating whether something is possible.

(53) Those silly fools think I'm going to die soon. I'm not. Shouldn't be surprised if I outlived the lot of them. And then we'll see! Oh, yes, then we'll see. Harold's got no children. Cedric and Alfred aren't married. Emma? Emma will never marry now. She's a bit sweet on Quimper but Quimper will never think of marrying Emma.

Will indicates that somebody is ready or willing to do something relating to the future.

(54) "I have a perfect recollection of the afternoon in question," replied Lady Westholme. "Miss Pierce and I {will, are willing to} do all we can to assist you." "Oh, yes," sighed Miss Pierce, almost ecstatically. "So tragic, was it not? Dead—just like that—in the twinkle of an eye!"

Note that with this meaning, *will* is permitted in *if* clauses.

(55) Sarah's thoughts came back from the past to the present. "I wonder," she thought, "if Dr. Gerard will let me talk to him about his work. He's done such marvelous work. If only he'll take me seriously ..."

Recall that *will* is usually not permitted in *if* clauses.

(56) I will give you some names and addresses of references **if** you {**want**, ***will want**} to know all about me.

Future Perfect

The future perfect tense refers to something that will happen at between the current time and a particular future time.

(57) a. Yet up-to-date information about who is bankrolling this effort will not be available until the end of January, by which point four states **will have voted** and Romney may have the nomination wrapped up.

b. "I know, dear, I know. But do try and be realistic about it. Your grandfather could cause a lot of trouble, you know. You're not of age yet. In another year you can do as you please. I expect Horace **will have come** round long before that."

shall

In British English, *shall* is used to express future time. This use is extremely uncommon in American English.

(58) a. When Virginia Gov. Robert F. McDonnell (R) asked antiabortion zealots in the General Assembly last week to soften the controversial ultrasound bill, he faced a dilemma in explaining his move: **Shall** I appear ill-informed or weak-willed?

b. When she **shall** die, take her and cut her into little stars. And she will make the face of heaven so light that all the world will be in love with night.

In British English, *shall* is used to make suggestions about what to do. This use is rare in American English.

(59) **Shall** we do the town?

Be going to refers to facts or events in the current situation as evidence for a prediction.

be going to

(60) "He's fond of him, is he?" said Craddock. "Used to be. Of course he was his daughter's child, not a son's child. That may have made a difference. And he had quite an affection for Bryan Eastley, Edie's husband. Of course, I don't know Bryan well, it's some years since I've seen any of the family. But it struck me that he **was going to** be very much at a loose end after the war. He's got those qualities that you need in wartime, courage, dash, and a tendency to let the future take care of itself. But I don't think he's got any stability. He'll probably turn into a drifter."

Be going to refers to somebody's intentions, or what they have decided to do.

(61) She told me she **was going to** stay with a rich lord in Scotland.

Note that the string of *going to go* is not allowed.

(62) I'm going (*to go).

Be going to expresses planned actions.

(63) He doubtless knows quite well that Allerton **is going to** meet Nurse Craven in the summerhouse tomorrow.

Vs such as {*hope, expect, intend, want*} indicate uncertainty about what will actually happen when they select *to* VPs as their complements.

Uncertainty

(64) Very simple. You cannot tell me now, but you **hope to** do so in a day or two. That means that you **want to** obtain the consent of the young lady. [unrealized future tense]

(65) cf. I **believe** him **to** be honest. [no future tense]

When *hope* selects a present simple tense clause as its complement, the sentence indicates future time.

(66) My best wishes to you all and I **hope** you **enjoy** meeting Tommy and Tuppence again.

Exercise 12

12_1

Select the expression that best completes each sentence:

(67) (Deciding, Having decided) to attend the concert, we bought four tickets for Saturday night.

(68) After (singing, having sung) the aria, Marian Norman received a standing ovation.

(69) Anthropologists believe these ancient cave dwellers to (live, have lived) somewhere north of the Red Sea.

(70) Only three Presidents (have graduated, graduate) from the military academies: Grant and Eisenhower from West Point, and Carter from Annapolis.

(71) The US Constitution stipulates that, to be eligible for the Presidency, a candidate must be a natural-born citizen, must (have lived, live) in the US for a minimum of 14 years, and must be at least 35 years old.

(72) All US presidents (have worn, weared, have weared) glasses, but some of these men didn't like to be seen wearing eyeglasses in public.

(73) By the time dinner was ready, I (did, had done) all my math homework.

12_2

Specify the time relation depicted by the underlined tense in each sentence, as illustrated in the example:

[e.g.] Tell me when you have finished. [future time]

(74) I'll write to you as soon as I have heard from Jenny.

(75) I would like to have won first place.

(76) Planning for the election, he decided what he should advocate.

12_3

Decide if the following sentences are correct. Correct the ones that are not. If they are correct, write "correct".

[e.g.] The roots of the plant had bursted the flowerpot.
[Answer: *had burst → burst*]

(77) After we've cut the grass, we'll weed the garden.

(78) The angry wasp stung me right on the end of my nose, and it hurted all afternoon.

(79) Sam spreaded his pita bread with hummus.

(80) It was so cold in the basement, the water had froze.

(81) Why have you came home so early?

(82) Our team has not beat them in three years.

(83) They never would have begun if you hadn't helped them.

(84) Has Gladys ever sang a cappella?

(85) We were torn between the two candidates.

(86) If we would have checked, we'd have known the store was closed.

(87) She laid another log on the fire to ward off the cold.

(88) Mrs. Ames was pleased that when the driver's test was taken by her son, he passed easily.

(89) The shoppers laid down their purchases carefully.

(90) Cindy retraced her steps and found the café at which she left her credit card.

(91) They would have liked to interview the astronauts.

(92) I had just laid down on the beach when it started to rain.

(93) Dan worked for this company for eighteen years, longer than any other current employee.

(94) When we saw the group perform, Julia, the lead vocalist, just broke her contract with a big recording company.

(95) If we had the chance, we would have stopped by your house.

12_4

Find errors and correct them in each sentence with respect to tense:

[e.g.] By the time we get to the picnic area, the rain will stop.

[Answer: *will stop* → *will have stopped*]

(96) I would have agreed if you would have asked me sooner.

(97) As a witness to the accident, Mary told what happened.

(98) Ever since he came to this country, he studied diligently.

(99) If they had enough money, they could have taken a taxi.

(100) As I thought about our argument, I was sure you lost your temper first.

(101) The clerk remembered that the manager has ordered the new shipment last Tuesday.

(102) How could I have forgotten that Great Britain included England, Wales, and Scotland?

(103) If Gary would have read the advertisement, he could have saved a hundred dollars on that camera.

(104) Walt would have done much better on the exam if he was present at our study sessions.

13
Hypothetical Situations

When Grammar Meets Linguistics

Conditional Clause

A conditional clause is a subordinate clause which expresses a condition or hypothesis about a situation. It typically begins with a subordinating conjunction such as *if*, *unless,* or *as soon as*.

(1) a. **If** you look after your health properly, you're all right anywhere.

b. You do hear the same story again and again **unless** you can manage to be quick enough and fend him off.

c. She decided that she would try to manage a little talk with Dr. Graham **as soon as** it could be managed.

Modality

Modals in (2) are used with other Vs to express ideas such as possibility, permission, or intention.

(2) can, could, may, might, shall, should, will, would, must, ought to, have to, used to, need, had better, dare

Classification

Conditionals are classified as *real conditionals* and *unreal conditionals* according to the degree to which they refer to real or unreal situations, respectively.

13.1 Real Conditionals

Real conditionals refer to real situations; i.e. things that are true, have happened, generally happen or are likely to happen. They are further classified as *generic conditionals*, *habitual conditionals*, *inference conditionals*, and *future conditionals*.

Generic

Generic conditionals refer to facts such as scientific truths.

(3) a. **If** water **is**n't absolutely incompressible, at least it compresses very little.

b. You may have noticed that **if** ice cream **has been** in the freezer too long it starts to taste funny.

Habitual

Habitual conditionals refer to situations or events that are generally true or happen often. In habitual conditionals, both main and conditional clauses have a present or present perfect tense. Habitual *if* is synonymous with *whenever*.

(4) a. **If** he **judges** it necessary, he **dispatches** a letter. He imitates some of the peculiarities of her handwriting in case she should think of taking his letters to the police.

b. They just give them some kind of pill out of a bottle and **if** they **don't get** better, they **try** a different pill.

c. The path they have taken depends on many chances. **If** they **have gone** alone, they **are** quite as likely to move in a circle.

Inference

Inference conditionals refer to situations or events that are inferred or concluded.

(5) a. "Have you thought enough about this, my dear?" he said at last. "There was no need to think long, uncle. I know of nothing to make me vacillate. **If** I **changed** my mind, it must be because of something important and entirely new to me."

b. "I hope," said he presently, "I have not been severe upon poor Mrs. Churchill. **If** she **is** ill, I should be sorry to do her injustice; but there are some traits in her character which make it difficult for me to speak of her with the forbearance I could wish."

c. I feel certain that **if** he **carries** anything heavy, he will drop it. It's really an agony to watch him.

d. **If** he **has** a conscience, he will suffer for his mistake. That will be his punishment as well as the prison.

Future

Future conditionals refer to future situations or events. They typically appear with instructions as in (6a), questions as in (6b), or suggestions as in (6c).

(6) a. "And you, maid Tess, you weren't well a day or two ago. This will make your head ache finely! Don't do any more, **if** you **feel** fainty; leave the rest to finish it."

b. The whole thing is fixed up. Definitely. If I pull this off, I shall be able to take a firm line with Uncle Matthew and **if** he **doesn't like** it, well, what do I care? It's adorable of you to be so interested in my long technical descriptions of the Albatross.

c. "I call that the fanaticism of sympathy," said Will, impetuously. "You might say the same of landscape, of poetry, of all refinement. **If** you **carried** it out, you ought to be miserable in your own goodness."

If *will* is used in the main clause, events are quite likely to happen in the future.

(7) Now, **if** your friends **have** any gratitude, they will say something pretty loud about you and me in return; but I cannot stay to hear it.

13.2 Unreal Conditionals

Unreal conditionals refer to unreal situations which are untrue or imagined and are less likely to happen. They are further classified as hypothetical conditionals and counterfactual conditionals.

Hypothetical

Hypothetical conditionals form an opinion or reach a conclusion on the basis of information that is not certain or complete about the present or the future.

(8) a. Certainly an efficient woman, thought the Inspector, and **if** she **murdered** a man she would probably murder him very efficiently, too.

b. **If** restitution **were** promptly made, he could hush the matter up.

In the following, the main clause has the future simple tense, and the conditional clause has the present or present perfect tense. Each sentence in (9) refers to something that probably takes place in the future.

(9) a. "For three years longer I must wander about; if I come back again, then we will celebrate our wedding; but if I do not, you are free, for I shall be dead. But pray to God that he will preserve my life."

b. And now, if you have quite finished, we will hark back to Kensington and see what the manager of Harding Brothers has to say to the matter.

In the following, the main clause has *would*, and the conditional clause has the past simple or past progressive tense. Each sentence in (10) refers to something that is unlikely to happen.

(10) a. As a kid, I decided that if our society dictated that one had to be black or white, I would be black.

b. If cutting-edge technology were king, Tintin (the 3D computer-generated film) would be ruling American shores, too.

c. We would never send a child home if that child was struggling with math.

d. They have been in prison so long that if the prison door stood open they would no longer notice! One of them, at least, no longer even wants to be free! And they would all be afraid of freedom.

If *should* is used in a conditional clause, there is greater uncertainty.

(11) If a bullet should strike the wall by my head, I would not investigate the matter!

Counterfactual

Counterfactual conditionals make assumptions about past events that did not happen or inconceivable states or situations in the present.

(12) a. Then I walked into the study and found the man shot. 'Who let him in?' 'I don't know. I think if my maid had done so, she would have told me.'

b. "No fingerprints at all," he said. "That means it has been wiped. Well, if there had been fingerprints, they would have told us very little. They would have been those of Mr. Ratchett or his valet or the conductor. Criminals do not make mistakes of that kind nowadays."

c. If Gore had won the 2000 election, we would all be driving cars that get 50 miles per gallon of gas.

d. We pray together, we tremble together, and we fall asleep. If the devil were to enter this house, he would be allowed to do so. After all, what is there for us to fear in this house? There is always someone with us who is stronger than we. The devil may pass through it, but the good God dwells here.

If I were you is used when you wish to give advice to somebody.

(13) Personally, if I were you, I shouldn't mention it to her.

13.3 Usage

Ellipsis + SAI

Alternatively, unreal conditionals are expressed with [missing *if* + SAI].

(14) a. I had no choice. Had I not come here, I would have been killed.

b. I have none of the usual inducements of women to marry. **Were** I to fall in love, indeed, it would be a different thing! but I never have been in love; it is not my way, or my nature; and I do not think I ever shall.

c. Van Helsing examines her teeth very carefully, whilst she is in the hypnotic condition, for he says that so long as they do not begin to sharpen there is no active danger of a change in her. **Should** this change come, it would be necessary to take steps!

If there is a present progressive tense in both main and conditional clauses, the sentence is ruled out.

(15) If you {hang, ***are hanging**} in there, you **are giving** yourself a chance.

Primary modals such as {*will, would, would have*} are usually not used in conditional clauses.

(16) a. Now, **if** you {permit, ***will permit**} me, we will converse quietly.

b. I said I would mention it to Mr. Wickfield, and **if** he {approved, ***would approve**}, as I had no doubt he would, I would come with pleasure.

c. **If** my maid {had, ***would have**} done so she would have told me.

Other primary modals can be used in both main and conditional clauses.

(17) a. **If** by any means I **can** delay this marriage, will you wait?

b. But even **if** the UN **could** act, Britain and France might not be keen on military action.

c. Furthermore, students don't want to thank a school for rejecting them, even **if** the rejection **may** be temporary.

d. Scientists investigate active volcanoes on the season premiere of "Nova", and experts discuss worst-case scenarios **if** a volcano **should** suddenly erupt.

In formal English, *were* is used instead of *was*.

(18) a. Then I saw, as though all the intervening time had been cancelled, and **I were** still standing in the doorway on the night of the departure.

b. Wherever he tours, crowds mob Mr. Abu Ismail as if **he were** a pop-star.

c. At any moment, even if **she were** cooking or cleaning, Mrs. Callahan might be summoned to pose.

13.4 Alternative Conditionals

unless

Unless means an exception to what you are saying. That is, *unless* means *if ... not*.

(19) Never, never will the grey cells function {**unless** you, **if** you do **not**} stimulate them.

as long as, so long as

{*as long as*, *so long as*} is used to say that one thing can happen or be true only if another thing happens or is true.

(20) a. I'm pretty much free **as long as** the head feels I'm effective at what I do.

b. But **so long as** the human brain is capable of recognizing this complex pattern it does not matter whether or not we have a theory that expresses it in physical terms.

Provided (= *provided that* or *providing*) is used to say that something will be possible only if something else happens or is done.

provided, providing

(21) a. For example, self- and peer-assessment may now be used in formal assessments of student work **provided that** the final judgment on any assignment remains with the teachers of a course.

b. The 1962 Treaty of Friendship with Western Samoa established an annual quota of 1500 migrants **providing** they were able to secure accommodation and employment guarantees.

The pattern of [{*I wish, If only*} + past simple V] indicates the regret about a present event.

I wish, If only

(22) a. **I wish** our opinions **were** the same.

b. **If only** you **knew** how I love you both!

The pattern of [{*I wish, If only*} + past perfect V] indicates the regret about a past event.

(23) a. David, **I wish** to God I **had had** a judicious father these last twenty years!

b. **If only** your grandparents **had come** to the United States instead of your parents.

The pattern of [{*I wish, If only*} + *could*] indicates that somebody was able to do something.

(24) a. Three hundred dollars is a power of money. **I wish** my mother **could** get it.

b. After Heidi had gone to bed that night, she lay awake a little while, thinking over everything the grandmother had said, especially about the joy the songs had given her. **If only** poor grandmother **could** hear those comforting words every day!

The pattern of [{*I wish, If only*} + *would*] indicates that somebody was willing to do something.

(25) a. That's good! **I wish** all the girls **would** leave, and spoil his old school. It's perfectly maddening to think of those lovely limes, sighed Amy, with the air of a martyr.

b. It went very slowly, but perhaps his father was able to see his good intentions as he did nothing to hinder him, in fact now and then he used the tip of his stick to give directions from a distance as to which way to turn. **If only** his father **would** stop that unbearable hissing!

as if, as though

{*as if, as though*} is used when something seems to be true, or something you imagine is not the real one.

(26) a. Notwithstanding that one may have evidence enough to believe that a person is guilty one is bound, if one is bound by it, to treat him {**as if**, **as though**} he **is** innocent.

b. We can estimate this time by comparing molecular sequences in the two species. Such estimates are by no means certain. There is, however, one famous case in which it is beginning to look {as if, as though} the molecular estimate is better than one based on fossils. This concerns the common ancestor of man and the great apes.

The pattern of [{*as if, as though*} + past tense] is used for emphasizing that something is not true. It describes a present event.

(27) a. Parents who send their children to private schools occasionally behave {as if, as though} they owned the faculty, {as if, as though} their amount of tuition were paying the faculty, each faculty member's entire salary.

b. New public management expects public agencies to behave {as if, as though} they were private ones, to organize themselves in terms of production principles which were highly relevant to the growth of industrial capitalism in the nineteenth century.

like

In informal English, {*as if, as*} can be replaced by *like*. As shown below, *like* takes an NP or an S as its complement. However, some speakers are reluctant to use *like* when it takes an S complement.

(28) a. It starts to look more like [$_{NP}$ a Victorian approach to welfarism] than [$_{NP}$ a bold new educational initiative].

b. %He explains the science behind a disc that looks like [$_{S}$ it's defying gravity].

Exercise 13

13_1

Select the expression that best completes each sentence:

(29) We asked ourselves what would happen if we (convenes, convened, would convene) advanced users of self-tracking technologies to see what we could learn from each other.

(30) Even if labor costs (are, can, could) a quarter of those in China to make a given product, the unreliability or unavailability of many components may make it uneconomic to make things elsewhere.

(31) But the reality is that, even if the economy (is, were, might have) to improve as a result, it would be many years before tax revenues return to where they were at the height of the bubble.

(32) There's often no way to know if a particular case (will, would) have been fatal if left untreated.

13_2

Decide if the following conditionals are correct. Correct the ones that are not. If they are correct, write "correct".

[e.g.] If I was you, I would apply for the scholarship. [Answer: *was* → *were*]

(33) Willis insisted that every employee is invited to the company picnic.

(34) Gloria was confused all day because it seemed as though it was Friday, but it was only Thursday.

(35) Vernon lost many of his friends because he acted as if he were better than they.

(36) We often complain about working too many hours; but if we were to work fewer, we would be complaining about smaller paychecks.

14 Nonfinite Clauses

When Grammar Meets Linguistics

14.1 Infinitive Clauses

Infinitive complements are nonfinite clauses with *to*; they optionally have an overt subject. Vs are sensitive to the type of infinitive complements.

In this pattern, the matrix V selects an NP and an infinitive clause. The understood subject of the infinitive clause is identical to the matrix object. PRO indicates an unpronounced pronoun. The Vs in (1) are called *object-control* Vs in the sense that the matrix object controls the understood subject of the infinitive clause.

+v, [SU ___ NP_1 [PRO_1 *to* VP]]

(1) advise, ask, encourage, invite, order, persuade, remind, teach, tell

(2) a. We **encourage** [prospective $authors_1$] [PRO_1 to follow HBR's *Guidelines for Authors* before submitting manuscripts].

b. This seems rather obvious, but apparently we should **remind** [ourselves$_1$] [PRO$_1$ to be decent to one another].

c. A leadership team at one of the companies we worked with **invited** [managers from across departments$_1$] [PRO$_1$ to participate in time-to-market new product teams].

+v, [SU$_1$ ___ [PRO$_1$ *to* VP]]

In this pattern, the matrix V selects an infinitive clause. The understood subject of the infinitive clause is identical to the matrix subject. The Vs in (3) are called *subject-control* Vs.

(3) agree, choose, decide, expect, hope, intend, learn, mean, offer, plan, promise, refuse

(4) a. No one$_1$ can **expect** [PRO$_1$ to live very long without experiencing a serious setback in his or her life or work].

b. He$_1$ **chooses** [PRO$_1$ to deal with conflict in private rather than in public].

c. Agreeing vociferously that CEO succession is in crisis, he$_1$ **offered** [PRO$_1$ to write an article about it].

+v, [SU$_1$ ___ (NP) [PRO$_1$ *to* VP]]

Some of subject-control Vs select an NP (which is optional) and an infinitive clause.

(5) a. Barney$_1$ **promised** (Robin) [PRO$_1$ to write a letter].

b. We$_1$ **offered** (shoppers) [PRO$_1$ to thank them for participating in the study].

+v, [SU ___ [NP *to* VP]]

In this pattern, the matrix V selects an infinitive clause. The underlying subject of the infinitive clause is overt. The shaded Vs in (6) are called *Exceptional Case-marking* (ECM) Vs.♣

(6) a. The Mariners drafted him in the first place largely because of his polish and because they **believed** [him to be closer to major league-ready] than anyone else of comparable talent in the draft.

b. Dennis was also wrong to **expect** [Harvey to clear away the opposition or even to point to its existence].

c. With that as a backdrop, the first thing Michael and his wife have to decide is whether they both **want** [him to build a career at Lafleur].

Some of ECM Vs select an infinitive clause in which *to be* may be missing.

+v, [SU ___ [NP (*to be*) XP]]

(7) a. They also **consider** [the violation itself (to be) more grave].

b. Danny **believed** [Tracie (to be) honest].

The following linking Vs select *to* VPs. They are called *raising* Vs.

+v, [___ *to* VP]

(8) appear, get, grow, look, prove, seem

(9) a. After giving his players time to enjoy a rare victory, he used the film session to point out the positives from the night before, then **looked** [to clean up the errors on the court].

b. He hadn't even graduated when he decided to set up his company, Customer Strategy Solutions, to develop software for order-fulfillment systems. That **proved** [to be a lucrative niche].

♣ Normally, a transitive verb assigns accusative Case to its object. But a verb like *believe, expect, require,* or *want* assigns accusative Case to the subject of its object clause. This looks exceptional. In this light, the term ECM was coined.

14.2 Gerund Clauses

Gerund complements are nonfinite clauses with V-*ing* forms. They optionally have a subject.

+v, [___ V-ingP]

The Vs in (10) select gerund complements.

(10) adore, avoid, delay, detest, dread, enjoy, fancy, favor, finish, like, mind, practice, recall

(11) a. But he **delayed** mak**ing** decisions and considered the relationships between these issues as he slowly moved toward the creation of a new business model.

b. Mr. Cote has also rebuffed suggestions that he might **fancy** do**ing** a big transformational acquisition which is just as well, given the market's memory of the big deals that brought the current Honey well into being.

c. Bob Fu **recalls** be**ing** a student protester at Tiananmen Square 23 years ago.

+v, [___ P V-ingP]

The prepositional Vs in (12) select gerund complements.

(12) agree on, burst out, can't help, can't stand, carry on, count on, decide on, end up, feel like, give up, go round, keep on, put off, set about

(13) a. But you shouldn't need a stress test to persuade yourself to improve your diet, **give up** smok**ing** and take your medication as prescribed.

b. One hint is the way Charalambous **set about** tam**ing** that quirky ceiling.

The phrasal prepositional Vs in (14) select gerund complements.

+v, [___ P P V-ingP]

(14) get away with, look forward to

(15) a. We will announce the specific date for our public unveiling event soon and **look forward to** shar**ing** our new brand identity with our fans.

b. As a slain brother's sister, I am thrilled about hoodie-wearing protesters recognizing Trayvon's humanity and support the thousands who demand that Zimmerman not **get away with** kill**ing** him.

Vs like *finish* or *deny* require the understood subject of the gerund complement clause to refer to the main clause subject.

Covert only

(16) a. I was so appalled by this lack of journalistic integrity that I_1 couldn't bear to **finish** [PRO_1 reading Henneberger's piece].

b. $Leaders_1$ of *Kind Hearts for Charitable Humanitarian Development* **denied** [PRO_1 being connected to terrorism] and sued the government.

Vs like *anticipate* or *advise* optionally select an overt subject. The understood subject of gerund complements may refer to the main clause subject as in (17a) or the listener or people in general as in (17b).

Covert or Overt

(17) a. $People_1$ **anticipate** [{PRO_1, our, your} giving rewards to partners who cooperate].

b. Some cats like privacy, and I always **advise** [{PRO, your} putting litter boxes in low-traffic spots in the home].

Possessive or Accusative

The overt subject of gerund complements could have either possessive or accusative forms. Accusative forms are popular in informal English.

(18) Tracie recommended [{his, him} applying for the job].

Accusative only

Vs such as *catch, keep,* or *find* permit accusative forms only.

(19) And with 75m American baby-boomers now on the threshold of retirement, there is a limit to what the country can afford to spend to keep {them, *their} going on and on.

14.3 Category-Selection

+v, [___ NP (*to*) VP]

Help selects the sequence of an NP and a VP with the optionally intervening particle *to*.

(20) Continuous, decision-focused strategic planning has helped [our top management team] (to) [streamline its agenda] and [work with business units and functional management] to make far better business-strategy and commercial decisions.

+v, [___ *for* NP *to* VP]

The following Vs select [*for* NP] and [*to* VP].

(21) appeal, arrange, ask, long, wait, wish

(22) a. Clinton appealed for countries in the region to fulfill the promise of reform offered by the Arab Spring.

b. I had it in our office standing at the foot of the stairs and I showed it to Mrs Topp, and arranged for her to take it out with her to Sydney.

The following Vs select [*to* VP] when they are passivized.

+v, [*be* ___ *to* VP]

(23) ask, believe, consider, know, report, say, think, understand

(24) a. Tenducci **is reported to** have lamented the loss of his wife.

b. Studies have shown that as the human brain **is asked to** process dizzying amounts of data, its ability to solve problems flexibly and creatively declines and the number of mistakes increases.

The following Vs select a wh-phrase and [*to* VP].

+v, [___ wh *to* VP]

(25) ask, decide, explain, forget, imagine, know, learn, remember, specify, tell, understand, wonder

(26) a. I just don't **know who to** trust anymore.

b. Then in the late 1960s, no one wanted to **be told what to** do any longer.

c. Companies in industries ranging from media to financial services to consumer goods are adopting systems that **specify when to** interact with customers as well as **what to** say to them.

The following Vs select an NP and an infinitival wh-clause.

+v, [___ NP [wh *to* VP]]

(27) ask, remind, show, teach, tell

(28) a. Have you **taught** your teens **what to** do when they witness discrimination?

b. Barney **shows** Ted **how to** use a video camera.

+v, [___ *to* VP]

The following Vs select [*to* VP] in order to show purpose.

(29) a. The Cliff Swallows **stopped to** migrate to the Mission at San Juan Capistrano, Calif.

b. In the mid-1960s, I **went to** work as a salesman for a real estate developer by the name of Valerio Cardinale.

+v, [___ {*to* VP, V-ingP}]

Some Vs select either infinitive or gerundive complements, with little or no difference in meaning.

(30) a. School was torture; unable to focus, he **hated** {to study, studying} and procrastinated endlessly.

b. NBC's Richard Engel reports from Athens, Greece, where government and financial 3 leaders **continue** {working, to work} to prevent an economic meltdown.

Vs such as *remember, forget*, or *try* create a difference in meaning, depending on the choice of nonfinite complements.

remember

[*Remember to* VP] means the remembering occurred before the action. [*Remember* V-ingP] means the remembering occurred after the action.

(31) a. I **remembered to** start my exhaust fan.
'I remembered I had the task and then did it.'

b. I **remembered** start**ing** my exhaust fan.
'I did the task and then remembered doing it.'

[*Forget to* VP] means that the subject did not carry out the action. [*Forget* V-ingP] means that the action occurred.

forget

(32) a. She said she had shopped there earlier in the day but **forgot to** buy two items.
'She didn't buy them because it slipped her mind.'

b. She **forgot** buy**ing** two items.
'She didn't remember that she bought them.'

[*Try to* VP] means that the subject attempted but did not necessarily carry out the complement action. [*Try* V-ingP] means that the subject carried out the action as an experiment.

try

(33) a. Greek leaders **tried** for a second day [**to** end an ongoing political crisis], under intense pressure to ensure (that) the country doesn't go bankrupt in the next few weeks and that it remains in the eurozone.
'They attempted to carry out the action of terminating an ongoing political crisis, but we are not sure about its success.'

b. He **tried** liv**ing** nearby so he could walk his daughters to school in the mornings.
'He performed the action of living nearby temporarily.'

Perception Vs select an NP plus either a VP or V-ingP. A bare infinitive complement just describes an action, but a gerund complement an *on-going* action.

+v, [__ NP {VP, V-ingP}]

(34) a. A witness **saw** them **capture** one man, and {**kick and punch**, **kicking and punching**} him as he was marched into the compound.

b. Joey **watched** Phoebe {**drown**, **drowning**} with her boyfriend.

+v, [___ NP V-ingP]

Vs such as *catch* or *imagine* select an NP plus a V-ingP form as their complement.

(35) a. An emotional Nixon was captured on several minutes of tape, saying at one point, referring to White House photographer Ollie Atkins, "I'm afraid he'll [**catch** me picking my nose]."

b. But it's a funnier and warmer book than that in the absurd chorus of the loudspeakers that broadcast the Dear Leader's lies, and in the nobility of individual North Koreans who remain decent and loving even as they suffer. [**Imagine** Charles Dickens paying a visit to Pyongyang], and you see the canvas on which Johnson is painting here.

+v, [___ NP *from* V-ingP]

Vs such as *prevent* or *keep* select an NP, *from*, and V-ingP as their complement.

(36) a. Parents are using smartphone apps and in-car cameras to [**prevent** their teenagers **from** engag**ing** in risky behavior].

b. A retired engineer's invention is [**keep**ing his community **from** becom**ing** climate refugees].

be used to V-ingP

When you *are used to doing something*, you are accustomed to doing it.

(37) My husband had worked digging graves with Herb since he was fifteen, and he [**was used to** tak**ing** orders].

(38) cf. He looks at how social media {is, ?are} used to {recruit, *recruiting} potential employees.

When you *used to do something*, you did it regularly in the past, but not any more.

used to VP

(39) Parents of harassed gay children **used to** be too ashamed to speak out.

Causative Vs select an NP plus a VP.

+v, [___ NP VP]

(40) Nothing **made** him change.

The V *let* selects an NP plus a VP, too. It permits somebody to do something.

(41) Mr. Helier had just voted to **let** employers refuse to pay for contraceptives and other services.

Exercise 14

14_1

Select the expression that best completes each sentence:

(42) Others have failed (duplicating, to duplicate) the classic toy, which is why every Slinky sold in the world is still made in the U.S.A.

(43) Zarrella reports you will be amazed when you see Orangutans (using, to use) iPads.

(44) A 26-year-old man plead guilty to child porn charges, (receiving, to receive) a 315 year prison sentence.

(45) Gruesome footage in China of a toddler falling victim to two successive hit-and-run accidents and then (being ignored, to be ignored) is galvanizing the nation, prompting a fierce debate over the state of morality in society.

(46) Armstrong talks about some online resources to help (teaching, teach, taught) your children to become computer-savvy adults.

(47) Matthew Chance reports that negotiations are crucial (avoiding, to avoid) another potentially divisive Greek election.

14_2

Select the expression that best completes each sentence:

(48) He noticed her (goes, go) out of the house.

(49) He smelled something (burning, burnt).

(50) He was seen (to look, look) out the window.

14_3

Select the expression that best completes each sentence:

(51) He helped her (going, to go) to see her parents.

(52) They bade me (carry, carried) the boxes.

(53) He will get them (cut, to cut) the tree.

(54) He was made (to leave, leave) the town by me.

Interjections!

[Words and Music by Lynn Ahrens]

When Reginald was home with flu, uh huh,
The doctor knew just what to do
He cured the infection
With one small injection
While Reginald uttered some interjections
Hey! That smarts!
Ouch! That hurts!
Yow! That's not fair,
Giving a guy a shot down there!

Interjections! Hey!
Show excitement. Ouch!
Or emotion. Yow!
They're generally set apart from a sentence
By an exclamation point
or by a comma when the feeling's not as strong.

Though Geraldine played hard to get, uh huh,
Geraldo knew he'd woo her yet
He showed his affection
Despite her objections
And Geraldine hollered some interjections
Well! You've got some nerve!
Oh! I've never been so insulted in all my life!
Hey! You're kinda cute!

15 Reported Speech

15.1 Structure of Reported Speech

The report structure is formed from a reporting clause and a reported clause.

(1) [$_S$ Brian **reports** [$_S$ Kodak once **handled** highly-enriched uranium to operate a special device at a production facility]].

In the following, the reporting clause and the reported clause are marked for a past tense.

(2) The president sued El Universo and one of its columnists last year over an article which **claimed** [that he **had told** troops to fire on a hospital during a police mutiny in 2010].

In the following, the present tense in the reported clause is to indicate that something is particularly important or true.

(3) He and his wife were told by doctors on Friday [that Children's Hospital of Philadelphia is considering a transplant for their daughter].

In the following, the present tense in the reported clause is to make a suggestion or give advice for the present or future.

(4) Mr. Stone pointedly told a group of delegates [that it is possible to have fair wealth distribution and fast growth at the same time].

In the following, the present tense for the reporting V is to express what somebody often says.

(5) Matthew Parris, who calls himself a Protestant atheist, says that Jesus was a man whose teachings have transfiguring energy.

In the following, the present tense for the reporting V is to indicate that what somebody said in the past is still important or true.

(6) My doctor says it's nothing to worry about.

In the following, the future tense for the reporting V is to predict what people will say or think.

(7) a. Skeptics will note that Fidel Castro opened up the island's economy a little in the early 1990s, after the collapse of the Soviet Union and the withdrawal of its subsidies.

b. The white moderate **will understand** that law and order exist for the purpose of establishing justice.

In the following, the embedded clause is a reported question (= indirect question).

(8) Swain wondered [why Syume would offer him cash when the businessman knew he had spent 17 years as a D.C. police officer].

{*if*, *whether*} is used to report indirect *yes/no*-questions.

(9) Indeed some are asking {**if**, **whether**} it is worth rebuilding the town.

Whether is used to highlight a choice of possibilities.

(10) The grueling test includes time in "Hogan's Alley," a mock street scene where candidates are confronted with surprise situations in which they must instantly decide, among other things, **whether** to shoot at a suspect.

The sequence of *whether or not* is grammatical. But the sequence of *if or not* is ungrammatical.

(11) The U.S. government has launched a new website and is pouring millions of dollars into two large studies examining {**whether or not**, ***if or not**} a drug can slow the progression of Alzheimer's among patients who are predisposed to the devastating disease.

15.2 Category-Selection

+v, [___ *that*-S]

The following reporting Vs select a *that* clause in order to make a statement.

(12) a. One group **complained that** the company was violating their freedom of choice.

b. He **decided that** every patient who came into the ER had to be seen by a qualified nurse within 60 seconds.

The reporting V *say* does not require the complementizer *that*. But the reporting Vs in (14) do not permit the omission of the complementizer *that*.

(13) Critics **said (that)** hardball meant playing dirty or mean, neither of which is true.

(14) a. Romney **answered *(that)** he would further lay out his positions as the November election approaches.

b. Some have **argued *(that)** NASA's failure to respond with appropriate intensity to the so-called foam strike that led to the accident was evidence of irresponsible or incompetent management.

c. Brown **replied *(that)** he could think of two possible explanations.

d. She **explained *(that)** monthly payments were skyrocketing on mortgages with adjustable interest rates.

+v, [___ (*to* NP) *that*-S]

The following Vs select an optional *to* NP and a *that* clause where the NP is a listener.

(15) a. We are exhausted and have **admitted (to** each other) **that** it's a struggle to be responsible parents.

b. At a critical moment in the lead-up to its IPO, Google used figurative language to great effect when it **announced (to** Wall Street's chagrin) **that** it would not report short-term earnings.

c. Prosecutors **suggested (to** potential jurors) **that** the hearings were material to Congress's concerns that children might be influenced by the conduct of professional athletes.

d. Smith recently **complained (to** acquaintances) **that** he suspected that Coleman had resumed a romance with an old boyfriend, the affidavit says.

The following Vs select an NP and a *that* clause where the NP is a listener.

+v, [___ NP *that*-S]

(16) a. Further testing, however, has **convinced** the team **that** Freeman's sight is better.

b. But Abdullah said (that) recent parliamentary elections in Egypt have **persuaded** at least some Israeli officials **that** the consequences of delaying peace could be more harmful in the long run.

c. The fungicide, linked in studies to a higher risk of liver tumors in animals, was found in trace amounts last month in products from Brazil after Coca-Cola, which owns the Minute Maid brand, **notified** the FDA **that** some Brazilian growers had sprayed their trees with the chemical.

d. In a five-hour event he hosted last week in a theater in a poor Caracas neighborhood, Chavez **reminded** his followers **that** past leaders provided hunger, misery, lead and death.

+v, [___ NP (*that*)-S]

Tell selects an NP and a *that* clause where the complementizer *that* is optional.

(17) We talked about strategies for increasing attendance, and after a while, I **told** the staff (**that**) I had some silly marketing ideas and was embarrassed to share them but was willing to do anything to help.

+v, [___ NP *to* VP]

The following Vs select an NP and *to* VP where the NP is a listener.

(18) advise, ask, beg, command, forbid, instruct, invite, order, persuade, remind, tell, warn

(19) Though the fund's overall assets constituted a tiny fraction of the firm's assets under management, she **asked** the board **to** review her tentative recommendation to limit the size of the fund.

+v, [___ (NP) wh-S]

The following V selects an optional NP and a wh-clause when it reports a question.

(20) She **asked** (him) **why** he'd wanted her to do something that bore no relation to her skills and experience, and he told her (that) it was to see how fast she could respond to the task.

Exercise 15

Select the expression that best completes each sentence:

(21) He (says, tells), "I have to go now."

(22) Ann (said to, told) me, "I can help you."

(23) She (said to, told) him that she was sleeping.

(24) I told him (that, if) I liked him.

(25) She told me that she (is, was) going to school.

(26) He told her that he (will, would) play tennis.

(27) She told him that she was washing the dishes (now, then).

(28) He told me that he (dreams, had dreamed) about me.

(29) She said that she had lost her bag (yesterday, the day before).

(30) My father said that he had heard from her (ago, before).

(31) He (told, asked) me when I would leave.

(32) Ann asked him (if, that) he had come to the party.

(33) She (told, said) him to come home early.

(34) She told him (washing, to wash) the dishes.

(35) He asked me (bring, to bring) him the newspaper.

(36) I ordered him (not, don't) to be late again.

(37) The doctor advised me not (smoke, to smoke) any longer.

A Noun is a Person, Place, or Thing

[Words and Music by Lynn Ahrens]

Well every person you can know
And every place that you can go
And any thing that you can show
You know they're nouns
A noun's a special kind of word
It's any name you ever heard
I find it quite interesting
A noun is a person place or thing.

Oh I took a train
took a train to another state
The flora and the fauna that I saw
were really great.
When I saw some bandits chasing the train
I was wishing I was back home again.
I took a train
took a train to another state.

Well every person you can know
Like a bandit or an engineer
And every place that you can go
Like a state or a home
And any thing that you can show
Like animals and plants or a train
You know they're nouns
You know they're nouns.

16 Passives

16.1 Typical Passives

Active

In active voice, the speaker focuses on a person or a thing that performs an action. The subject is a performer or an agent of the event described by the main V.

(1) Gibbons's inability to manage his subordinates **caused** a problem.

Passive

In passive voice, the speaker focuses on a person or a thing affected by an action. The passivized V group takes the string of [*be* Past-Part.]. The subject is a patient or a theme of the event described by the main V.

(2) Of course, one could argue that the problem here **was caused** by Gibbons's inability to manage his subordinates.

Progressive

For the progressive passive tense, the V group takes the string of [*be being* Past-Part.].

(3) Born November 22, the polar bear cub **is being fed** by zookeepers because his mother could not produce milk.

In the following, the V group takes the string of [modal *be* Past-Part.].

(4) He laments his self-absorption and his bad temper, though he finds out that some of his moods are symptomatic of what his doctors have diagnosed as Graves disease, an auto-immune disorder that **may be caused** by stress.

In the following, the V group takes [modal *have been* Past-Part.] in order to talk about the past time.

(5) Apple executives **must have been delighted** when Mike Daisey, the playwright and star, recently retracted his nastiest allegations about the mistreatment of workers making Apple's products in China.

Infinitive

Note the passive infinitives: [*to* {*be, have been*} Past-Part.].

(6) a. "The gele is my trademark," says the Nigerian finance minister, Ngozi Okonjo-Iweala, describing the colorful head wrap she puts over her short, graying hair before she allows pictures **to be taken**.

b. But currency specialists say that the yen's fall appears **to have been given** more momentum by the recent commitment of the Bank of Japan (BOJ) to buy government bonds until it gets close to a new 1% inflation goal, as well as by a record trade deficit in January.

Subjects of passive sentences may be direct objects (as in 7a), indirect objects (as in 7b), objects of Ps (as in 7c) or clausal complements (as in 7d) in the corresponding active sentences.

Surface Subject

(7) a. **The Mumbai plot** was led ___ by Lashkar-i-Taiba but funded by the ISI and inspired by al-Qaeda.

b. **The state** was given ___ an overall grade of B-plus by Education Week, which publishes the annual report.

c. **One building** was slept in ___ by about 700 evacuees.

d. **That homosexuality is "innate"** was added _____ by the Board of Education.

Short (= agentless) passives do not have an agent *by* phrase.

Short

(8) After Ollanta Humala became Peru's president last July, his first anti-drugs chief, Ricardo Soberon, a former activist in NGOs, announced a surprise suspension of coca-eradication efforts, but without putting any other policies in place. Mr. Soberon **was sacked**.

Short passives are used when the agent is unknown.

(9) A federal judge has awarded $50 million to a Florida couple after their son **was killed** in an unidentified bombing in Israel.

Short passives are used when the speaker does not want to make the agent known.

(10) All this coincided with the political infighting in which Mr. Lage **was ousted**, during which all financial and budgetary discipline was blown away, according to a foreign businessman.

Short passives are used when the agent is understood.

(11) He would need coalition partners, among them hardline Islamist conservatives who share his anti-Americanism and agree with him that the way Osama bin Laden **was killed** last year was Pakistan's greatest humiliation.

Long

Long passives have an agent *by* phrase. The agent phrase is forced when the agent carries important new information.

(12) Only later he remembered the stillness of her breathing, and understood all that must have been passing in her sweet, precious heart while she lay beside him, not stirring, in anticipation of the greatest event in a woman's life. At seven o'clock he was waked **by the touch of her hand on his shoulder, and a gentle whisper**. She seemed struggling between regret at waking him and the desire to talk to him.

Given-New

The Given-New Contract dictates that old information should come before new information. The long passive in the following is an instance of this contract.

(13) He pulled up the blind and rang the bell loudly. **It** was at once answered **by the appearance of an old friend, his valet, Matvey, carrying his clothes, his boots, and a telegram**.

End-Weight

The End-Weight Principle dictates that long and complex phrases should occur at the end of the sentence. The long passive in the following is an instance of this principle.

(14) In the morning she was waked by a horrible nightmare, which had recurred several times in her dreams, even before her connection with Vronsky.

In long passives, the instrument is realized with a PP headed by *with*.

with

(15) a. She was beaten with a club.

b. Santorum had raised more than $3 million after doing well in Iowa, and Wood suddenly was gifted with money to rent office space and $15,000 to pay a temporary staff.

c. She was raised with a sense of duty that prevented her from agreeing to a divorce when William asked for one.

Stative Vs cannot be passivized because they do not affect the object in active voice.

Non-Stativity

(16) a. These early works contained themes and artistic styles that would stay with him.

b. *Themes and artistic styles were contained by these early works.

(17) a. The biggest rock weighs more than two pounds.

b. *More than two pounds is weighed by the biggest rock.

(18) a. Irish resembles other Celtic languages.

b. *Other Celtic languages are resembled by Irish.

Multiword Most of multiword Vs do not permit passivization: inseparable phrasal Vs (e.g., *come across*, *fall for*), permanently-separated phrasal Vs (e.g., *get ... down*, *see ... through, tire ... out*), and phrasal prepositional Vs (e.g., *get along with*, *put up with*).

(19) *Ugly women were never fallen for ___ by handsome men.

(20) Let the kids run around in the garden, and {that'll soon tire them out, *they will be soon tired ___ out by that}.

(21) *Barney was put up with ___ by Ted.

Dative The indirect object of *for* dative Vs (e.g., *bake, catch, find, buy*) cannot be the subject in the passive sentence.

(22) a. They found [$_{NP}$ her] [$_{NP}$ a nice apartment].
b. *She was found a nice apartment (by them).
c. A nice apartment was found for her (by them).

(23) a. John gave [$_{NP}$ Mary] [$_{NP}$ a book].
b. Mary was given a book (by John).
c. A book was given to Mary (by John).

get *Get* passives have the string of [*get* Past-Part.]. They are more informal than *be* passives.

(24) I sometimes get scared of growing up because I really love being young, being little.

Get passives are not permitted with cognition Vs.

(25) He could not look people in the eye when in conversation, possessed no sense of humor, was delinquent and paranoid, and {was known, *got known} by all as 'The Madman'.

16.2 Pseudo-Passives

The string of [*be* Past-Part.] does not always indicate passive voice. Some past participles function as As. Adjective

(26) a. Though she professed to be tired from her rigorous interview, the Nigerian economist's voice was filled with energy and urgency when she addressed the bank's need for speed.

b. It is our responsibility as Black activists, radicals, and socialists to create vibrant new leadership that offers a real alternative to [$_{NP}$ the tired civil rights establishment] and to the bankrupt two-party system.

Passives in complements following *get* and *have* have a causative meaning. +v, [___ NP V-*ed*]

(27) a. He was supposed to be a guy whose oratory really [got the party excited].

b. Now let's really focus and [get this problem sorted out].

(28) a. He could not have [had such legislation passed] through a Democratic legislature.

b. Mr. Skvorecky often ran afoul of the country's Communist authorities, and before leaving Czechoslovakia in 1969, he had lost jobs and [had many of his works banned].

Happenstance

Happenstance passives refer to unfortunate events or something that happens by chance.

(29) a. Obama had spent much of the year locked in negotiations with Republicans over the national debt, with little to show for the effort but a sagging approval rating.

b. Ted got his car towed away last night.

Concealed

Concealed passives are productive in British English. They are not true passives in that there is no passive Aux.

(30) a. Unlike other surgical weight-loss procedures like gastric bypass or the gastric sleeve, Lap-Band surgery does not require cutting or stapling the stomach, making it up to 10 times safer than those more invasive surgeries.
'... does not require the stomach to be cut or stapled ...'

b. She wanted them selected by the "30 Americans," renowned African American artists whose work is part of a major exhibit at the Corcoran Gallery of Art.
'She wanted them to be selected ...'

c. The ink cartridge and paper need replacing.
'The ink cartridge and paper need to be replaced.'

Exercise 16

16_1

Change the following active sentence into the corresponding passive one:

(31) You will retain all of the components of the active verb string.

(32) I should probably give the mechanic a tip.

(33) MBC is interviewing all of the candidates tonight.

16_2

Change the following passive sentence into the corresponding active one:

(34) Many lives have been saved by the discovery of insulin.

(35) The indelible marker was invented by Sidney Rosenthal in 1952.

(36) According to the National Graffiti Information Network, four billion dollars in damage to public property is caused annually by vandals.

(37) Magic markers are now being manufactured by Binney & Smith, Inc.

Rufus Xavier Sarsaparilla

[Words by Kathy Mandry, Music by Bob Dorough]

Now I have a friend named Rufus Xavier Sarsaparilla
and I could say that Rufus found a kangaroo
That followed Rufus home
And now that kangaroo belongs
To Rufus Xavier Sarsaparilla ...
Whew! I could say that, but I don't have to
Because I have pronouns I can say,
He found a kangaroo that followed him home
And now it is his
You see, *he, him* and *his* are pronouns
Replacing the noun Rufus Xavier Sarsaparilla,
A very proper noun,
And it is a pronoun replacing the noun kangaroo.
(How common.)

Now Rufus has a sister named Rafaella Gabriela Sarsaparilla
If she found a kangaroo I'd say to you
She found a kangaroo that followed her home
and now it is hers but I can't say that
Because she found an aardvark
That fell in love with her and they're so happy.

17 Modals

When Grammar Meets Linguistics

17.1 Modality

Modality

Modal Vs express modality such as possibility, probability and certainty, ability, permission, instructions and requests, suggestions, offers and invitations, wants and wishes, obligation and necessity.

Modality is the attitude of the speaker to the hearer or to what is being said.

Classification

Modals can be classified into three categories according to their forms.

(1) a. Primary modals
can, could, may, might, must, shall, should, will, would

b. Secondary modals
dare, need (to), have to, ought to

c. Semi-modals
be going to, be supposed to, be allowed to, be bound to, be certain to, be likely to, be sure to, be able to, had better, had best, have got to

Modals can be classified into three categories according to their basic meanings.

(2) a. Ability, Permission, Possibility
can, could, may, might, be able to, be allowed to

b. Advice, Necessity
must, should, ought to, dare, need (to), had better, had best, have to, have got to, be bound to, be supposed to, be certain to, be likely to, be sure to

c. Future Time
will, shall, would, be going to

Ordering

When you have several Auxes, modals should be the first Aux.

(3) a. The attacks **must have been** anticipated, but Romney appeared less comfortable with handling them.

b. Thomas Jefferson **may have been** relaxed about such matters, but no modem candidate for the presidency would dare to profess no faith, or to question the existence of the Almighty.

c. The woes of its debt-ridden neighbors **might be** hurting Germany now.

Modals have only one form.

(4) Your advisor {**can**, ***cans**, ***canning**} help you choose alternative investments that fit your needs.

Modals do not normally refer to the time when something happens. There are a few exceptions.

Future

{*will, shall*} refers to a future event or situation.

(5) a. The first round **will** be held on May 23rd and 24th, with run-offs scheduled for mid-June.

b. But tomorrow I **shall** be sober.

Past

Could is used as the past form of *can* when the latter refers to ability.

(6) When a cruel stroke robbed him of speech in 1998, he found he **could** still compose cantatas for sales reps to sing. And he **could** play the drums.

Would is used as the past form of *will* when the latter refers to a future event or situation.

(7) Scott told his local paper he wasn't even sure who he **would** vote for the next day.

Contraction

In spoken and informal written English, *will* and *shall* are contracted as '*ll*, and *would* as '*d* after ProNs.

(8) a. I'm not sure he**'ll** be there.

b. If he got up earlier, he**'d** get to work on time.

However, they are never shortened at the end of a sentence.

(9) a. Yet it requires much forbearance on the part of the electorate to accept that the candidate will not do half the things he has said {he will, *he'll}.

b. Would he not try to balance the federal budget, even though he has said {he would, *he'd}?

Compare (9) with the following.

(10)	a.	Yes, I am.	cf.	*Yes, I'm.
	b.	No, I am not.	cf.	No, I'm not.
	c.	No, it is not.	cf.	No, {it isn't, it's not}.

In the following, note that '*d* is contracted from *had*.

(11) They'd voted for the parties.

Negation

Negative words immediately follow modals.

(12) a. The comments should not be construed as a recommendation of any individual holdings.

b. If Conservatives cannot woo black and Asian voters, they may never win majorities again.

Not after the modal *can* must be spelled as *cannot*.

(13) The reality is that a body of religious and moral beliefs {cannot, *can not} cohere, or spread, without people to care for it.

There is an exception: *can not only* A *but also* B.

(14) The league discourages the use of unsupervised doggy doors, which **can not only** lead to lost pets **but also** allow wildlife into a home.

Contraction

In spoken and informal written English, modals and *not* can be contracted.

(15) a. I **couldn't** get water without bribing local bureaucrats.
b. You **mustn't** stay here.
c. The doctor said I **shouldn't** smoke any more.
d. I **wouldn't** advise him to change anything.

There are irregular short forms.

(16) a. This inspection **shan't** include a review of the substantive content of the incoming mail.
b. These reforms **won't** solve all our problems, but if they had been in place earlier, this crisis would have been much less damaging to the United States.
c. I **can't** identify any popular literary trend that didn't originate online.

The following contraction is sometimes used.

(17) a. Someone in our family **mightn't** be alive.
b. You **oughtn't** play games you're bound to lose.

The following contraction is very rarely used.

(18) I don't see why we **mayn't** at least go hunting further along.

Question

In questions, the modal is fronted.

(19) a. **May** you ___ hold this for me, please**?**

b. What else **might** I ___ be able to do for them**?**

You cannot have two primary modals in a clause.

(20) a. *They **will can** achieve their symbolic goals.

b. They **will be able to** achieve their symbolic goals.

Alternatives

Some of primary modals have alternative phrasal expressions (i.e., semi-modals).

(21) a. O'Brien was adamant that he **is able to** handle both jobs. [= can]

b. As populations age and health-care costs increase, there **is likely to** be a greater emphasis on monitoring, prevention and maintaining wellness in future, with patients taking a more active role. [= might]

17.2 Ability, Permission, or Possibility

Can refers to ability, permission, possibility, admonition, speculation, disbelief, offer, etc. *can*

(22) a. Your advisor **can** help you choose alternative investments that fit your needs. [ability]

b. Students **can** take a year away from university. [permission]

c. While nothing is finalized, it is possible that we **can** reach an agreement that will accomplish all those things. [possibility]

d. Make sure they **can** be stored overnight in a discreet location. [admonition]

e. Other economic data and news **can** be found on pages 104-105. [speculation]

f. He **can't** beat them. [disbelief]

g. I have a car. I **can** take Rene to the station. [offer]

Could refers to ability (in the past), permission, possibility, speculation, regret, disbelief, suggestion, offer, etc. *could*

(23) a. He **could** run faster than anyone else. [ability]

b. After that, foreigners **could** invest more freely in Chinese shares, bonds and property. [permission]

c. His approach is more sophisticated, and does not require separate sub-pixels for each of the three primary colors to produce a full-color image, which **could** improve the screen's resolution. [possibility]

d. The deal between North Korea and America is good and **could** even turn out to be great. [speculation]

e. I'm sorry, I **couldn't** come yesterday. [regret]

f. It **couldn't** have been Jim! He'd never do something like that. [disbelief]

g. A new business model **could** help people in poor countries light their homes cheaply using solar power. [suggestion]

h. So far this has not proved popular. Cremation **could** provide a solution. [offer]

{*Could you, Would you*} is used in formal situations and sounds very polite. *Could you* is more polite than *Would you*.

(24) a. How **could you** justify that opinion?

b. What **would you** do in this situation?

The pattern of [*could have* Past-Part.] indicates that something **was likely to** happen in the past, but it **did not** happen.

(25) a. Cash **could have been invested** to boost the economy.
'But it wasn't invested.'

b. Or maybe he **could have induced** PIXAR Studios to make an animated children's movie about these birds, with voice-overs by Michelle Pfeiffer, Sylvester Stallone, and Bernie Mac.
'But he didn't induce PIXAR Studios.'

may

May is used to show possibility, permission, etc.

(26) a. You **may** be quite sure, my dear Hastings, that financial gain is the first thing for which I look. [possibility]

b. "Hello, **may** I speak with Ellen?" she says, tapping a pen on a long list of names. [formal permission]

May as well is used to suggest a sensible action.

may as well

(27) Have we enough chairs? Then we **may as well** sit down and talk in comfort.

Might is used to show possibility, speculation, suggestion, criticism, permission, etc.

might

(28) a. Unless domestic interest rates are liberalized first, to give savers a reason to keep their money in the Chinese banking system, China's financial system **might** fall apart. [possibility]

b. On the other hand, this type of mercurial diplomacy is just the thing Mr. Kirn **might** have learned at his father's knee. [speculation]

c. For your own sake, though, you **might** want to impose sanity rules on yourself. [suggestion in a very polite way]

d. One obvious problem with their reasoning was that, although equities **might** have beaten bonds over most long periods, the horizon of the average investor is much shorter. [criticism]

e. **Might** I offer you a little glass of cherry brandy? [old-fashioned, permission in formal requests]

Might as well is used to suggest a sensible action.

might as well

(29) If we're going to do this, we **might as well** do it right.

Be able to refers to somebody's ability to do something.

be able to

(30) Coach Marvin Lewis declined to say how much the rookie **was able to** do in practice, but said he thought Dalton was up to date on the offensive plan for Sunday's playoff game against Houston.

Be able to can be selected by a modal, V-*ing*, V-*en*, or *to* VP.

(31) a. Simultaneously, the company **would be able to** build a payment record of its clients, sorting the unreliable from the rest.

b. Some investors confess that there is social cachet in **being able to** tell people that they are involved in fun sectors such as music.

c. Over the years Goldman has **been able to** navigate quietly around its problems.

d. The trick is that, **to be able to** use the electricity, the system's keeper must buy a scratch card on which a reference number is printed.

be allowed to

Be allowed to refers to permission.

(32) Every Friday, employees **were allowed to** wear casual clothes to work, which may have contributed to more casual behavior, such as less formality in meetings, no strict adherence to specified break times, and more personal conversations in the hallways.

Be allowed to can be selected by a modal, *-ing*, *-en*, or *to* infinitive.

(33) a. The Chinese prime minister criticized China's big banks for acting like a monopoly and said private capital **should be allowed to** flow into the finance sector.

b. Besides, nuclear plants are long-lived things. Today's reactors were mostly designed for a 40-year life, but many of them are **being allowed to** increase it to 60.

c. Through language we have **been able to** pass on stories of past heroes and enemies, warn future generations of failed philosophies, create new ideals for better living, share our aspirations and fears, even express our wonder at all that remains unknown to us.

d. If the vote to override the NCAA's proposal fails, schools will continue to be allowed to offer multi-year scholarships, as they have since October.

The pattern of [{*could, may, might*} *have* Past-Part.] indicates a possibility that something happened in the past, but you are **not certain** if it actually happened.

(34) a. The federal civil rights charges against Anthony McIntosh, 48, come more than three years after 19-year-old Ronnie White was found strangled in the Prince George's County jail. White's death was ruled a homicide by the medical examiner, but a state police investigation later concluded that White could have killed himself.

b. If so, they may have quarrelled, and he may have killed her in a fit of rage.

c. A New York City school custodian might have saved a 6-year-old boy from harm when he intervened after a man pretending to be the boy's uncle grabbed the child's hand.

The pattern of [{*might, could*} *have* Past-Part.] indicates that if a particular thing had happened, then there was a **possibility of something else** happening.

(35) a. Two years ago, Stone Brewing made a video announcing a new product called *BrewDog/Stone Luciferin Golden Imperial Stout*, a strong golden ale brewed with coffee and cacao nibs to

mimic the flavor of a much-deeper-hued beer. Only 2,000 bottles were packaged, each with a blindfold attached so buyers could conduct their own blind tastings and surprise their friends. A few news services **might have picked up** the item, but if they had checked the dateline, April Fool's Day, they would have known they were being pranked.
'But they didn't pick up the item.'

b. Mr. Khan, who has been in U.S. custody since 2003, pleaded guilty to five counts of violating laws of war, including murder and attempted murder; if convicted at trial, he **could have faced** life behind bars.
'But he didn't face life behind bars.'

17.3 Advice or Necessity

must

Must refers to necessity, obligation, prohibition, probability, insistence, etc.

(36) a. Any artificial enhancement was unfair, they complained, and **must** be eradicated. [necessity or obligation]

b. The prospect of an Asian arms race is genuinely frightening, but prudent concern about China's build-up **must** not lapse into hysteria. [prohibition]

c. In 2008, 51 people applied for asylum in Serbia. Last year the number was 3,134. The true figure crossing into Serbia **must** be several times higher. [inferred probability]

d. Any suggestions for the places to visit in Prague? In Prague, you **must** visit a few galleries. [polite insistence]

{*Cannot*, *Can't*} is used when you are fairly sure that something is not the case. You do not use {*must not*, *mustn't*} with this meaning.

(37) Yet British public opinion {cannot, #must not} be ignored entirely.
'I am convinced that British public opinion is not ignored entirely.'

The string of [*must have* Past-Part.] is used when you are **almost certain** that something has happened.

(38) When puppeteer Paul Zaloom was in fourth grade, he must have been the funniest kid in the cafeteria.

Should is used to indicate advice, probability, reproach, etc.

should

(39) a. He should use it to encourage large businesses. [advice]

b. The Gancia brand is popular in Italy but faces slim margins and weak growth. Russian control should boost sales in Russia and could help relaunch Gancia in America, Britain and Germany, where it was strong 40 years ago. [probability]

c. In the face of continuing problems, that should have been fixed a long time ago. [reproach]

Ought to is used to indicate advice, probability, reproach, etc.

ought to

(40) a. "Spanish should be included in commercials shown throughout America. Every American child ought to be taught both English and Spanish," says Mario Obledo, president of the League of United Latin American Citizens, which was founded more than a half-century ago to help Hispanics learn English and enter the American mainstream. [advice]

b. After leaving the presidency, Washington continued to explore and find success in new lines of business, such as whiskey production. The Mount Vernon Estate is just outside Washington. Perhaps Mr. Cohen ought to pay it a visit. [inferred probability]

c. "There was a pattern in some companies, a handful of them, of leaving them with enormous debt and then within a year or two or three having them go broke," Gingrich said. "I think that is something he ought to answer." [reproach]

The pattern of [{*should, ought to*} *have* Past-Part.] is used to express a **mild obligation** to do something in the past, but it **was not done**.

(41) a. Some say Mr. Miliband should have tried harder to find a fresher candidate than the former mayor, who stands accused of insensitivity to the Jewish community and of strenuous efforts to minimize his tax liability.
'You had a mild obligation to try harder, but you did not.'

b. By the way, you ought to have turned that over to the police at once.
'You had a mild obligation to turn it over to the police, but you did not.'

The pattern of [{*should, ought to*} *have* Past-Part.] is used when you are **fairly sure** that something has happened.

(42) a. The body, if there is a body, ought to have been discovered by now, or will be very soon.

b. The return of Vladimir Putin to the Russian presidency ought to have caused the Obama administration to reshape its policy toward the Kremlin. Putin based his election campaign in large part on anti-Americanism; he has increasingly pursued policies contrary to vital U.S. interests, such as his military support for the Syrian regime of Bashar al-Assad and his threats against NATO's European missile-defense system.

dare

Dare is used to indicate advice, admonition, impossibility, etc.

(43) a. **Dare** I talk against Baxter, especially as he mourned the death of his second son? [advice]

b. You **dare** not cause problems for everyone else. [admonition]

c. I **dare** not tell my mother about this. [impossibility]

Dare selects [___ (*to*) VP]. In the following, *dare* is used as a main V in that it appears with either *not* or a modal V.

(44) a. We **did not dare** to oppose him, fearing that if we did not do as he said, he would denounce us.

b. I **would dare** to die for him.

In the following, *dare* is used as a main V in that it is conjugated with -*s* or -*ed*: *dares* and *dared*.

(45) a. She **dares** to judge from her observations based on memory and experience that Wentworth is not really in love with either of the Musgrove daughters, nor they with him.

b. Humbleby **dared** to oppose me over the water scheme.

In negative or interrogative sentences, *dare* selects bare infinitives. In this case, it behaves like a (modal) Aux V.

(46) a. That's why I **daren't let** her know about me and Pamela.

b. How **dare** you **bomb** my city**?**

In negative sentences, *dares* or *dared* selects [*not* V]. In this case, *dare* is between a main V and a (modal) Aux V.

(47) a. With the threat of layoffs ever-present, she **dares not complain** about this modern-day slave labor.

b. Many Japanese soldiers and civilians realized the generals were leading their country to disaster, but **dared not speak** out.

need (to)

Need (to) is used to indicate necessity, advice, etc.

(48) a. The first thing we **need to** know is whether America or Israel intends to attack their nuclear facilities, and if so when. [necessity]

b. But if he really does end up taking a different path from his father, then he will **need** vast amounts of foreign support. [advice]

{*Don't need to, Haven't got to, Needn't*} is used to express no obligation or necessity to do something.

(49) a. You **don't need to** stand atop the Galata tower to see problems ahead.

b. After all, I **haven't got to** get back here to England by a given date, or anything like that.

c. The George W. Bush administration took such action belatedly a few years ago, resisting it even after wars in Iraq and Afghanistan were underway; we **needn't** repeat that mistake.

The string of [{*need not have, needn't have*} Past-Part.] indicates that somebody did something that was not necessary.

(50) Had he done his duty in that respect, Lydia {need not, needn't} have been indebted to her uncle.

had better or *had best*

{*Had better, Had best*} is used to indicate advice.

(51) a. Whoever wants to know the heart and mind of America **had better** learn baseball.

b. We **had best** turn into this inn to consider what plan to adopt, and also to dine, for it is now time.

Had better not is the negative form of *had better*.

(52) I told him he **had better not** do that again if he knows what's good for him.

have to

Have to is used to indicate necessity, obligation, probability, insistence, etc.

(53) a. Rather than simply pointing out the perpetrator, witnesses are asked how confident they are when identifying him. And they **have to** make up their minds quickly. [necessity or mild obligation]

b. Under new euro-zone rules the budget deficit will have to be cut from 5% of GDP last year to below 3% by 2013. [inferred probability]

c. You have to consider your health. [polite insistence]

Must not ≠ *do not have to*. *Must not* means that 'it is important that you do not do it.' *Do not have to* means that 'it is not necessary for you to do it, but you can do it if you want.'

(54) a. Any euro-zone scheme must not undermine the EU's single market in financial services, which includes non-euro countries like Britain.

b. You don't have to wait for me. I can get a taxi home.

Must refers to obligation and necessity in the **present** and the **future**. *Had to* refers to obligation and necessity in the **past**.

(55) But he had to spend a lot of cash to hold on to a state he would once have expected to win easily.

{*Do*, *Does*, *Did*} is used to make a question involving {*have to*, *not have to*}.

(56) a. Why do you always have to lay your problems at my doorstep?

b. Don't you have to wait for him?

You do not normally form questions like (57) by putting a form of *have* before the subject.

(57) *How often have you to buy petrol?

Have to is used in various contexts. It can be selected by a modal, *-ing*, past morpheme (*-ed*), or *to* infinitive.

(58) a. You **will have to** examine horribly smashed faces and very extra dead bodies a good deal.

b. I'm very sorry for **having to** bother you.

c. He has **had to** revise this design.

d. You are not likely **to have to** respond to such a monumental problem.

have got to

Have got to is used instead of *have to* in informal English.

(59) We just **have got to** keep him under control through the rest of the season.

However, *had got to* is not used.

(60) He {**had to**, ***had got to**} undergo emergency surgery.

be bound to

Be bound to is a semi-modal V. It means 'certain or extremely likely to happen.'

(61) Mr. Bezos **is bound to** be the target of more criticism as his company's hefty investments in new areas continue to put a dent in its bottom line.

be supposed to

Be supposed to is used to indicate mild obligation.

(62) Parliament has only just begun to debate the composition of the body that **is supposed to** draft the constitution.

be{certain, likely, sure}

Be {*certain, likely, sure*} selects {*to* VP, *that*-S}.

(63) a. There **is certain** **to** be plenty of talk about Goodell's suspensions imposed last week.

b. Jim Prideaux and his boss, Control, are both working for the British intelligence service MI6 in 1973, when the Cold War is at its height, and Control **is certain** **that** MI6 has been infiltrated by a mole.

17.4 Future Time

will

Will is used to indicate future time, volition, probability, request, offer, certainty, etc.

(64) a. The first round **will** be held on May 23rd and 24th, with run-offs scheduled for mid-June. [future time: prediction]

b. If you like to send your police doctor to see me, I **will** give him my views. She was unable to be present at the inquest for the same reason. [volition]

c. If we unlock the keystone, I am certain we **will** discover a map that indicates we have moved in the proper direction. [inferred probability]

d. James, **will** you carry this tray into the dining room? [request]

e. I **will** give you some names and addresses of references if you want to know all about me. [offer]

f. It's been three years since you were called away. You **will** always continue to live on in our hearts. We love you and we miss you so much. [certainty]

Shall is used to indicate future time (in British English), volition, suggestion, offer, etc. *shall*

(65) a. I **shall** be leaving early in the morning, but I want to tell you how struck I have been by your ability. [future time: prediction]

b. But rest assured, my dear colleague, we **shall** do our best. [volition]

c. **Shall** we do the campus? [suggestion]

d. **Shall** I shut the door? [offer]

Would is used to indicate **future** time in the **past**, a regular action in the **past**, a hypothetical result, probability, a polite request, etc. *would*

(66) a. He thought that that **would** give him time to tell Prince Rainbow. [prediction in the past, future in the past]

b. In an emergency she **would** always behave like a frightened child. [regular action in the past]

c. Anyway, if you love someone, you **would** take the risk. [hypothetical results]

d. He went down the stairs. I hesitated and then went along the other wing towards my own room. The little man **would** be expecting me. [inferred probability]

e. **Would** you please tell me which way I ought to go from here? [polite requests]

The string of [*would like* {*to* VP, NP}] is used to express what somebody wants. *would like*

(67) a. Biologists **would like** [to understand how they do it].

b. They would like [greater influence on the writing of the constitution] from civil society.

{*Would not like*, *Wouldn't like*} is used to express what somebody does not want.

(68) a. I can quite understand the feelings lying behind this, and would not like [to try and influence you in any way].

b. But if it was possible, I wouldn't like [it] much.

The string of [*would like to have* Past-Part.] means that somebody **wishes now** that something had happened in the past, but it did not happen.

(69) Bert shivered: he would like to have put his jacket on, but that was out of the question at a job like this.

The string of [*would have liked* {*to* VP, NP}] means that somebody **wanted** something to happen, but it did not happen.

(70) a. He said no more. Mary Dove once more turned away, but this time, he thought, she went rather unwillingly as though she would have liked to know more of what was in his mind.

b. He had had, on the whole, a very good life. It was a pity it was going to be over so soon, that was all. But at any rate he had had, he supposed, everything worth having. Except a son. He would have liked a son. He would like to know now that he had a son living after him.

In short, *would like to have* expresses '**present wishes** about past events.' *Would have liked* expresses '**past wishes** about past events.'

The string of [*I would like you to* VP] is used if somebody in authority wants to tell somebody to do something.

(71) Tres bien. Now, you understand, something of importance has arisen. I would like you to come and see me at once.

The string of [*I would like*] selects {*to* VP, NP} in order to make a request.

(72) a. There is something. Dr. Graham, I would like to ask you.

b. I would like your advice on that point, Doctor.

The string of [*would you mind* V-*ing*] is used to make a request.

would you mind V-ing

(73) In that case, would you mind my drinking from your cup instead of from mine?

The string of [{*would hate, would love, would prefer*} {*to* VP, NP}] is used to express wants and wishes.

would {hate, love, prefer}

(74) a. Your wife would hate to think of you amusing yourself in London.

b. You would hate the books I read and the music I loved.

would{rather, sooner}

The string of [{*would rather, would sooner*} VP] is used to indicate that somebody prefers one situation to another.

(75) a. I **would rather** discuss how to increase our trade than how to decrease it.

b. When once they had done this, they **would sooner** or later realize that the privileged minority had no function.

Usage

{*Could you, Will you, Would you*} is used to tell somebody to do something. {*Will you, Would you*} is used by people in authority.

(76) a. I hope this doesn't cramp your style, but **could you** please not hum while you work?

b. **Would you** like us to sort through your things ourselves, box them up, give your clothes to Goodwill, and pick and choose what to keep? Or **will you** do this the next time you are home?

c. Mr. Ewell, **would you** tell us in your own words what happened on the evening of November twenty-first, please?

be going to

Be going to is used to indicate future time.

(77) A change is coming. A great wind **is going to** blow.

Exercise 17

17_1

Select the expression that best completes each sentence:

(78) We wanted to (have avoided, have to avoid) any controversy.

(79) The debate about guns is no longer over whether assault rifles ought to be banned, but over whether guns (shall, will, should, would) be allowed in bars, churches and colleges.

(80) With the threat of layoffs ever-present, she (dares, is dareing, dares to) not complain about this modern-day slave labor.

(81) He thought he (was, will be, would be) bound to be a baker.

(82) Before the latest decision, Jon Storck, Grace Fellowship's pastor, was worried what his congregation would do if it (have to, had to, must) leave the school.

(83) It's an Amazon jungle out there. Local shops and booksellers (have best, had best, should have best, must have best) up their game if they want to stick around.

17_2

Decide if the following sentences are correct. Correct the ones that are not. If they are correct, write "correct".

(84) We would have preferred to have eaten Chinese food.

(85) You should never have lain your radio near the edge.

(86) When I enter college, my parents will be married thirty years.

(87) I should have liked to have met them.

Verb: That's What's Happening

[Words and Music by Bob Dorough]

A verb expresses action, being or state of being
A verb makes a statement
Yeah, a verb tells it like it is.
Verb! That's what's happening!

I can tell you when it's happening
Past present future tense
Tell you more about what's happening
Say it so it makes some sense
I can tell you who is happening
Verb you're so intense
Hey! Every sentence has a subject
Noun person place or thing
Find that subject, where's the action
Verb can make the subject sing
Take the subject, what is it? What?
What's done to it? What?
What does it say?
Verb! You're what's happening!
I can question like, What is it?
Verb! You're so demanding!
I can order like, Go get it!
Verb! You're so commanding!
When I hit I need an object!
Verb, hit! Hit the ball!
When I see I see the object!

18 Clauses

When Grammar Meets Linguistics

18.1 Relative Clauses

Relative ProN

The relative ProNs are *that* (for humans and inanimate things), *who* and *whom* (for humans), *which* (for inanimate things), and *whose* (possessive form for humans and inanimate things).

Attributive Usage

Attributive (= defining, restrictive) relative clauses give information that helps to identify the person or thing you are talking about.

(1) And even people who have spent their lives working, saving and planning—people who have done everything right—are worried about the future.

If the antecedent is [+human], the relative clause is introduced by *that* or *who*.

(2) a. Then he withdrew with the air of a man {that, who} has done his duty and dealt successfully with a tiresome member of the travelling public.

b. If in doubt, look at how it is done in America. Then sort out the electoral registers: you need tough registration requirements for the voters {who, that} dislike you.

If the antecedent is [-human], the relative clause is introduced by *that* or *which*.

(3) a. Their battle was never about policy; it was sparked by the bad blood {that, which} simmered between them.

b. Mrs. McGillicuddy handed the porter his tip {which, that} he received with disappointment, clearly considering it more applicable to third-class than to first-class travel.

Subject Relative ProN

In the following, *that, who,* or *which* plays the role of a subject in the relative clause. The subject relative ProN cannot be missing.

(4) a. Mr. Rudd resigned abruptly as foreign minister on February 22nd, spurred by opinion polls *(that) said Labor's only chance of winning the next election in 2013 was if it restored him as leader.

b. Kirill Rogov, a columnist *(who) is one of the protesters' ideological voices, says this may be one of the movement's strengths.

c. Resettling her hat *(which) had slipped askew, she sat up and looked out of the window at what she could see of the flying countryside.

Object Relative ProN

In the following, *that, who,* or *which* plays the role of an object in the relative clause. Note that *that, who,* or *which* can be missing when it is the object of the V in the relative clause.

(5) a. The Press roundtable talks about the role (**that**) the same-sex marriage issue plays ___ in the upcoming presidential election.

b. The lady (**who**) you met ___ last week lives next door.

c. The Democrats have made their choice for 2012, but Republicans are only beginning their nominating process. While their hearts may long for a firebrand, their heads should tell them that come 2013 they'll need someone to govern, a task (**which**) Obama is especially ill-suited for ___.

The relative ProN can play the role of the object of a P. When the relative ProN is the object of a P, it can be missing.

(6) a. So you see, it might have been the train (**that**) your friend saw Bryan in ___.

b. Do you know the person (**who**) you remind me of ___?

c. His eyes passed idly across the room to his bookcase (**which**) he reserved ___ for various thrillers, works of detective fiction and an occasional volume of science fiction.

Usage

In formal English, *whom* is used instead of *who* as an object of the V in the relative clause.

(7) He thought of a man {**whom**, **who**} he had passed ___ in the street a few weeks back.

In formal English, the P always goes in front of {*whom, which*}.

(8) a. You accept things too easily at their face value. You always have done. You accepted quite easily the fact that it was Judith **to whom** Allerton was talking ___ in the summer house.

b. He wrote an excellent novel in the manner of Edgar Allen Poe, which was inexplicably refused publication by all the publishing houses **to which** he sent it ___.

Whose is used at the beginning of a relative clause to show who or what something belongs to or is connected with.

(9) A hospital expansion project in San Jose, Calif., has been halted after constructions crews unearthed more than 1,000 coffins filled with the bodies of people **whose** families couldn't afford proper burials.

Relative Adverbial

Adverbial relative clauses are introduced by {*when, where, why*} rather than by relative ProNs.

(10) a. I saw him for the first **time when** lunching here yesterday.

b. The taxi drew up with a jerk at the quiet **hotel where** Anne Morisot was staying.

c. Of course, if you had proper food and clothes and hadn't to work more than a reasonable number of hours every day, there is no natural **reason why** you should not live for another fifty or sixty years.

Consecutive Usage

Consecutive (= non-defining, non-restrictive) relative clauses are relative clauses that merely add information about the Ns they modify.

In writing, they are set off by commas. In speech, they are set off by pauses and falling intonation at the end of the clause.

(11) a. Let me see, you are Mr. Bryan Eastley, the husband of Miss Edith Crackenthorpe, who died five years ago.

b. He turned to the woman on the sofa, who was sitting with a piece of scone and honey in her hand, quietly appraising him.

They can modify proper Ns.

(12) "Not this time," said John, who had caught up his rifle.

They can be stacked.

(13) The blackbirds were genuine enough. They were put there by someone, who knew about the old business, who wanted revenge for it.

Reduction is not possible in consecutive relative clauses.

(14) She rose to her feet and replaced the cotton gloves, *(which) she had twisted ___ entirely off in her anguish.

In consecutive relative clauses, *which* can refer to the whole situation described in a main clause.

(15) She was a little tense, which was understandable.

That is not used in consecutive relative clauses.

(16) He took no faintest interest in the police court proceedings, {which, *that} in any case were purely formal.

Attributive vs. Consecutive

An attributive relative clause identifies the N it modifies. A consecutive relative clause, separated by commas or pauses, adds information about the N it modifies.

(17) a. The students who attended class regularly will do well on their exam.
'The students who will do well are only those who attended regularly.'

b. The students, who attended class regularly, will do well on their exam.
'All the students attended class regularly and all will do well.'

(18) a. The students who had to take exams are tired.

b. The students, who had to take exams, are tired.

what

What can be used as an alternative to *which* and *that* in nonstandard dialects.

(19) Obediently Trefusis pulled the heavy black curtains across the window. Poirot switched on the light {what, which, that} was masked by a big alabaster bowl hanging from the ceiling.

Resumptive ProNs are inappropriately used in a relative clause, appearing in the original position of the relative pronoun.

(20) But the knife that was found in the well corresponds very closely with the knife wounds that he suffered {∅, *them, *it}.

Extraposed relatives are relative clauses that have been moved away from the Ns they modify.

Extraposition

(21) a. A book **which was written by Chomsky** appeared.

b. A book appeared **which was written by Chomsky**.

(22) a. Powerful software **that can turn computers into a microphone and camera** has been discovered.

b. Powerful software has been discovered **that can turn computers into a microphone and camera**.

Stacking of relative clauses regularly occurs in spoken English.

Stacking

(23) He added: "The president has a very bad record on the issue of abortion and children **who are disabled** **who are in the womb**. I think this simply is a continuation of that idea."

Reduction of subject relatives occurs by omitting the relative ProN and a following form of *be,* leaving a present participle, a past participle, or an A followed by a PP.

Reduction

(24) a. She sat down in the chair (which was) **facing Miss Marple**.

b. Next day Sugaino dispatched a light truck up the road (which was) **manned by four men of his military police**, to search these trucks and to interrogate the drivers and the guards, and anybody else who might have knowledge of the matter.

c. She added the teapot and the kettle to the big silver tray and carried the whole thing through to the library where she set it on the small table (which was) **close to the sofa**.

Free Relative

Free relative clauses stand alone rather than modifying a head N. There are two types: definite free relatives and indefinite free relatives. Definite free relatives are introduced by *what, where*, and *when* as in (25). Indefinite free relatives are introduced by *who(m)ever, whichever, whatever, wherever* and *whenever* as in (26).

(25) a. Well, tell us **what** you do remember.

b. Michael knows **where** the well is, but he won't tell me.

c. I had been about a week in Baghdad when I ran across him and he asked **when** I was leaving the Kelseys.

(26) a. Caris noticed that Petranilla did not anticipate trouble with obedient Alice, who would probably marry **whomever** they picked for her.

b. Both stipulate that the expiration date for prescription drugs is the one stamped on the package by the manufacturer or one year after a drug is dispensed, **whichever** comes first.

c. It forces me to look around **wherever** I am now.

d. **Whenever** you can use analogy, **whenever** you can explain one thing in terms of another, you should try it; an analogy often breathes new life into an otherwise ordinary comparison and contrast passage or essay.

18.2 Participle Clauses

Participle clauses give more information about an N or an NP.

(27) a. President Obama's re-election campaign has released new ads **attacking Mitt Romney's record at Bain Capital** by looking at his record with GST Steel.

b. A panel of scholars dissect a booming trend in child-rearing: So-called "attachment parenting," popularized in part by parenting gurus like Dr. William Sears.

Perception Vs may select an NP followed by a V-*ing* form.

+v, [___ NP V-ingP]

(28) a. He saw Johnson playing a key role as head of the CEEO in efforts to pass legislation prohibiting discriminatory hiring practices by federal agencies and private businesses with federal contracts.

b. You may have heard your parents talking about the elections that are going on now, but it's a little strange because no one around here seems to be voting.

18.3 Appositive Clauses

Some Ns such as *rumor, danger, impression,* or *comment* select a *that* clause as their appositive complement.

(29) a. In his new book, Fulsom recycles an outlandish rumor that Nixon conspired with the mafia to have JFK killed.

b. As companies grow, there is a danger that novel ideas get snuffed out by managers' desire to conform and play it safe.

c. As Russian observers noted, all plausible opposition candidates were barred in advance, creating the impression that there was no alternative to Mr. Putin.

d. They talk about former President Bill Clinton's comments that hiking taxes on the rich alone isn't going to solve the country's economic problems.

18.4 Time Clauses

The V in a time clause has a **present** or a **past** tense.

(30) a. Compromise would anyway be impossible while the war is a living memory.

b. Here are the top movies Friday through Sunday, with estimated weekend receipts and total receipts since each movie opened.

c. He takes a look at security measures going into place before the Olympic games begin.

A future tense is not used in a time clause.

(31) You'll never find Mrs. Lancaster till you {find, *will find} Mrs. Johnson.

as, when, while

{*As, When, While*} shows that two events happen at the same time.

(32) a. Author Ronald Scott and Pulitzer Prize-winning journalist Janny Scott join the Melissa Harris-Perry panel as they discuss the impacts of President Obama's mother, Ann Dunham, and Mitt Romney's mother, Lenore, on their political lives.

b. When he had winked the tears out of his eyes, he suddenly discovered that he was hungry.

c. He spun round just in time to see Mrs. Parsons dragging her son back into the doorway while the boy pocketed a catapult.

Reduction

In a time clause, the subject and *be* can be missing.

(33) a. When (he is) giggling, the anchor must be high.

b. Arcalaus the magician gave him more than two hundred lashes with the reins of his horse while (he was) tied to one of the pillars of a court.

(*Ever*) *since* indicates a situation which started from a particular time in the past and continued until a later time. In the following, the main clause has the past perfect tense, while the time clause has the past simple or past perfect tense. *since*

(34) a. His death was a result of severe chronic obstructive pulmonary disease (COPD), congestive heart failure, and he had suffered from Alzheimer's disease since he was 70 years old.

b. It had been years since his client had attempted to collect the award from Bales.

In the following, a situation started in the past and still continues now.

(35) a. It's been five months since the lien was imposed.

b. Yes, I have been reading it ever since I woke.

18.5 Purpose and Reason Clauses

To infinitive clause is an instance of purpose clauses. *to* VP

(36) To get a sense of how cultural expectations of mothers differ in countries like France and the United Kingdom, Chris Hayes talks with Pamela Druckerman, journalist and author of *Bringing Up Bébé: One American Mother Discovers the Wisdom of French Parenting*.

{in order, so as} to

{*In order to, So as to*} selects bare infinitives.

(37) a. The assumption is that Amazon is trading short-term profits **in order to** establish its dominance in the booming e-book market.

b. He thought also of hurrying to the Community Centre and staying there till the place closed, **so as to** establish a partial alibi for the evening.

{*In order not to, So as not to*} selects bare infinitives.

(38) a. Sometimes when teachers speak loudly, the students just speak louder **in order not to** be bothered by the interruption.

b. He kept the house blinds drawn **so as not to** see the Jewish protesters circling silently outside.

{so, in order} that

The shaded conjunction introduces a purpose clause.

(39) a. Volunteers in Mr. Obama's re-election campaign will use social-media tools **so (that)** they can work conveniently from home rather than in a dingy field office.

b. If necessary, I could cable her to tell her his address **in order that** she might not leave Australia without seeing him.

Avoidance

Purpose clauses of *avoidance* express a thought, feeling, or idea that the purpose for doing something is to stay away from an undesirable outcome.

(40) a. She stepped back **for fear of** being in the company of a ghost.

b. She stepped back **for fear that** she would be in the company of a ghost.

(41) A young pig named Pinkeye was given the task of tasting all his food before he ate it, **lest** it should be poisoned.

Reason

Reason clauses are used to explain why something happens. They are introduced by conjunctions such as {*because, since, as, for, now that, seeing that, inasmuch as, (just) in case*}.

(42) a. It will be a happy occasion **because** she will be with old school friends she rarely sees any more.

b. No. 1 Platform was not at the moment unduly crowded **since** a train had just gone out.

c. His smile continued **as** he remembered a story he had once heard concerning Anthony Trollope, the novelist.

d. But their efforts were rewarded, **for** the harvest was an even bigger success than they had hoped.

e. **Now that** the John Edwards trial is going to a jury, she says anything can happen.

f. **Seeing that** the woman standing in the doorway was moving to go, he shouted to her.

g. He had no hope that a day would bring any relief to his suffering, which he believed would last forever, **inasmuch as** he was enchanted.

h. I keep my tablet PC in my bag, of course, **(just) in case** I need it.

18.6 Result Clauses

{so, with the result} that

Result clauses are used to indicate the result of an action or a situation. They are introduced by conjunctions such as {*so, so ... that, such ... that, with the result that*}.

(43) a. If you opt to remove it, slide a small knife beneath the membrane to cut it enough **so (that)** you can grab it with your hands and pull it off.

b. Unfortunately, the critics have concentrated all too much on Golding's debt to Christian sources, **with the result that** he is popularly regarded as a rigid Christian moralist.

{so, such} ... that

{*so...that, such...that*} indicates the result of an action or a situation.

(44) a. Bachmann looked good but never **so** good **(that)** people started asking how much the clothes cost or if they came from a fancy store or designer.

b. Nonviolent direct action seeks to create **such** a crisis and foster **such** a tension **(that)** a community which has constantly refused to negotiate is forced to confront the issue.

such (a(n)) (A) N

When *such* modifies an N, the indefinite article *a(n)* and an A can intervene.

(45) a. Jordan Crawford and Maurice Evans stood frozen as Lin dunked and screamed with **such excitement** that the bandage on his chin came loose.

b. The undulating fabric created by interlacing vertical threads by hand is **such laborious work** that a skilled weaver could only produce four inches per day.

c. Wandering farm animals were **such a nuisance** that in 1827 a fence was erected around the Capitol to keep cattle out.

So can modify either an A or an Adv.

so {A, Adv}

(46) a. Why are Americans apparently **so hostile** to the model of government-supported child care that has taken hold throughout the rest of the industrialized world?

b. Betty Towle, a missionary teacher, redheaded and **so ugly** that no one ever had a puppy crush on her, made me stay in for recess fourteen days straight.

The pattern of [*too* {A, Adv} *to* VP] indicates that a situation does not happen because somebody or something has an excessive amount of a quality.

too {A, Adv} *to* VP

(47) a. It is still **too** early **to** forecast success, but on a recent weekday afternoon Marshall Courts and Seven Oaks were quiet and peaceful.

b. Germany can offer lessons in how to get back into shape, but the essence of its model is rooted **too** deeply **to** be copied with ease.

The pattern of [{A, Adv} *enough to* VP] shows that a situation happens or is possible because somebody or something has a sufficient amount of a quality.

{A, Adv} *enough to* VP

(48) a. Such remarks do nothing to sway Mr. Bezos, who is convinced that rapid technological change creates huge opportunities for companies **bold enough to** seize them.

b. Winston just hadn't seen many first-year players mature quickly enough to make dramatic impacts.

Enough can be used as a prenominal modifier.

(49) I wanted to make enough money to buy a sports car.

18.7 Concession Clauses

Contrast

Concession clauses convey a contrast with the content of the main clause. Clauses introduced by {*although, though*, *even though*} present information that makes the main clause content unexpected. Clauses introduced by {*while*, *whereas*} simply express a contrast.

(50) a. {Although, (Even) though} one catches nothing, it's nice.

b. The others wanted empires and were engaged in building them, {whereas, while} he had only ever wanted the union of all the Greek peoples.

Emphasizer

{*Still, Nevertheless, Just the same*} adds an emphasis to the contrast.

(51) a. Although house prices are still edging lower, both sales and construction are rising.

b. Although his company is profitable, it nevertheless needs to face up to some serious problems.

c. Although she hated them, she agreed to help them just the same.

In the pattern of {*despite the fact that*-S, *in spite of the fact that*-S}, *that* can be missing.

{*despite, in spite of*} *the fact* (*that*)-S

(52) a. The soldier shouted at them in German, demanding to know who they were, but neither boy replied, **despite the fact (that)** they had mastered the language, and could speak it as well as their mother tongue.

b. Achilles could never catch up with a tortoise he was following, **in spite of the fact (that)** he traveled ten times as fast as the tortoise.

18.8 Manner Clauses

As is used to show how somebody does something, or how something is done. {*Just, exactly, Precisely*} is used before *as* for emphasis.

as

(53) a. He holds it **just as** you would hold a dagger you were going to stick into someone.

b. It looked almost **exactly as** it had looked before.

c. He found that here, **precisely as** in Russia, there were rich men who owned everything.

{*As if, As though*} shows that the information in the manner clause might not be true.

as {*if, though*}

(54) a. I am beginning to feel **as if** the whole of the country is full of nothing but homes for the elderly!

b. She pushed out a hand behind her **as though** blindly seeking for support.

{*the way, in the way*} (*that*)

{*The way (that), In the way (that)*} shows how somebody does something, or how something is done.

(55) a. She would run home, run every step of **the way that** would bring her closer to Tara and to Mother.

b. I was working in England, in an office at books **in the way that** women have to work in my country, because as you know, I am a poor woman and I have had to work all my life to earn my living till I find a husband who suits me.

how

How is used to show the manner in which somebody does something.

(56) He asked me **how** I was going back to England. Flying? I said no, I wasn't flying, I was going by sea.

18.9 Subject Clauses

Subject clauses are subordinate clauses that play the role of a subject of sentences.

Infinitive

Infinitive subject clauses are clauses that have [*to* VP]. They may occur with or without a visible subject preceded by the complementizer *for*.

(57) a. **For them to realize what it is they have seen** takes a little while.

b. **To have too much power** is bad for her.

Gerund subject clauses have a V in *-ing* forms. They may include a possessive N or possessive ProN as their subject.

Gerund

(58) a. **Victor's eating all the salted almonds** was disgusting.

b. **Having recourse to murder** is stupid.

That clauses, which function as a subject, are introduced by the complementizer *that* and include a modal or tensed V.

that

(59) a. **That nothing should be touched** is most important.

b. **That she had given birth to two such big sons** is amazing.

Interrogative (embedded question) clauses, which function as a subject, begin with a *wh*-element and include a modal or tensed V.

Interrogative

(60) a. Her life and her reason almost have been shaken by the blow which has fallen on her. **Whether she will rally** is very doubtful.

b. **How a crime affects the lives of people who are quite outside it** is interesting.

Subject clauses are used to make a connection to previous discourse and to introduce a new topic.

New Topic

(61) My father-in-law has been brutally murdered, and unless a case can be made out against the most likely suspect for robbery and murder, it seems that one of his own family killed him. **To bring that person to justice** will mean bringing shame and disgrace on us all ... If I am to speak honestly, I must say that I do not want this to happen.

Extraposition

The rule of *extraposition* moves a clause in subject position to the end of a sentence, substituting an expletive *it*. Compare (62) with (60). Extraposition sentences are much more frequent than subject clause sentences. They are used to move heavy clauses to the end, in keeping with the End-Weight Principle.

(62) a. Her life and her reason almost have been shaken by the blow which has fallen on her. It is very doubtful whether she will rally.

b. It is interesting how a crime affects the lives of people who are quite outside it.

Extraposition applies to {*that*, infinitive, interrogative} clauses, but only infrequently to gerund clauses.

(63) a. It is most important that nothing should be touched.

b. It is amazing that she had given birth to two such big sons.

(64) a. It takes a little while for them to realize what it is they have seen.

b. It is bad for her to have too much power.

(65) a. It is so confusing when you assume the character of a male detective.

b. It was not clear whether Ralph and Alan had inflicted fatal wounds on one another or someone else had been involved.

(66) a. It was disgusting Victor's eating all the salted almonds.

b. It is stupid having recourse to murder.

A few Vs such as {*appear, develop, happen, seem, turn out*} can appear only in the extraposition pattern with *that* clause.

(67) a. It appears that it is not a castle but an inn.

b. *That it is not a castle but an inn appears.

Exercise 18

18_1

Select the expression that best completes each sentence:

(68) Adjective clauses that begin with one of the relative pronouns are called (prepositional, relative) clauses.

(69) The following italic word group is a (dependent, independent) clause: If most car accidents occur within 5 miles of home, *why doesn't everyone just move 10 miles away*?

(70) The independent clause in a complex sentence is called the (subordinate clause, main clause).

(71) (Adjectival, Subordinating) conjunctions link an independent clause to a dependent clause.

(72) The conjunction *unless* shows (time, condition).

(73) The conjunction *although* shows (contrast, result).

18_2

Select the expression that best completes each sentence:

(74) Black reports on the feeling by some (that, who) Russia may be the only country that can stop the Syrian slaughter.

(75) Human beings (who, whom) are the most fascinating species on earth, are also the most admirable.

18_3

Select the expression that best completes each sentence:

(76) Reza Sayah reports on the sudden rise of cases of women (attacking, attacked) men with acid in Pakistan.

(77) New York man files a class action lawsuit against Apple (claiming, claimed) its SIRI ads are deceptive.

(78) Sylvester reports on the latest cruise liner accident—an engine fire on a ship (carrying, carried) 1,000 people.

(79) A Navy jet (crashing, crashed) into an apartment complex in Virginia Beach, Virginia, (sending, sent) flames and thick black smoke into the air. At least six people were hurt.

(80) Kaman and Martin have teamed up to build an (unmanning, unmanned) helicopter they hope will save lives in war zones.

18_4

Put every word in parentheses in the right place in the sentence: (Sometimes it is used twice.)

(81) But is it much ask it open up its markets, as it demands of others? (too, to)

(82) The stock has seen heavy gains in recent weeks many investors can't afford not to have Apple in their portfolio. (such, that)

(83) Even minuscule quantities of steroids were to trigger a reaction which could then be detected. (enough)

(84) There is much information available online today a student can practically write a paper on a book without even opening it. (so, that)

18_5

Underline every conjunction in each sentence:

(85) Seeds were removed from cotton bolls by hand until Eli Whitney invented the cotton gin.

(86) Eli Whitney invented not only cotton gin but also the interchangeable part.

(87) Nowadays we take the idea of interchangeable parts for granted, but it was a revolutionary concept at that time.

(88) For example, when a rifle is constructed with interchangeable parts, a defective part can be replaced quickly and easily with an identical piece.

18_6

Underline the relative clause in each sentence. Add a comma if necessary.

[e.g.] Margaret Mitchell who wrote *Gone with the Wind* was an Atlanta newspaper reporter.

[Answer: Margaret Mitchell, <u>who wrote Gone with the Wind</u>, was an Atlanta newspaper reporter.]

(89) The heroine of the story is Scarlett O'Hara who is a willful, defiant, manipulative Southern belle.

(90) The movie that was made from the novel won ten Oscars and has become a classic.

(91) Mitchell was born in Atlanta where she lived her entire life.

18_7

Rewrite each of the following sentences, recovering missing expressions:

(92) Andrew reports on the historic visit of Aung San Suu Kyi to Thailand and the work she's doing while there.

(93) Maktabi reports on the Syrian National Council's new leader, a Kurdish activist living in exile in Sweden.

18_8

Underline every postmodifier in the following sentences, providing its POS:

[e.g.] The teenager <u>who lives across the street</u> (Adjective Clause) rakes the leaves <u>in our yard</u> (PP) for a reasonable price.

(94) Marcus knows that man who is waving to us.

(95) The lumber industry in the Pacific Northwest, which always fluctuates with the economy, was a victim of the recession that occurred in the late 1980s.

(96) My father, who hates yard work, paid the man mowing the lawn an extra bonus.

18_9

Join the two sentences to make one sentence, changing the second sentence into an appositive phrase:

[e.g.] Aunt Rachel loves her job. She's a butcher at Daegu.

[Answer: *Aunt Rachel, a butcher at Daegu, loves her job.*]

(97) I have heard that the crew cut is coming back in style. That haircut was the hallmark of the 1950s.

(98) The deepest part of the ocean is located in the Western Pacific near the island of Guam. It is the Marians Trench.

(99) During its annual migration, the golden plover flies from the Arctic to Argentina. This bird is an amazing navigator.

18_10

There are four instances of comma missing from this passage. Can you put them back?

(100) Noam Chomsky an emeritus professor of linguistics at Massachusetts Institute of Technology and a well-known political activist critical of U.S. foreign policy traces modern-day American imperialism to its earliest roots 25 years before the American Revolution and he explains how the United States has lived up to its reputation as "the most frightening and dangerous country in the world."

19 Discourse Effects

19.1 Nonreferential *It*

Nonreferential *it* appears in the subject position. It is a type of **expletive** subjects. In the following, the ProN *it* is nonreferential (or impersonal). Nonreferential *it* expects new information; it talks about times, dates, the weather, or the situation.

Expletive

(1) a. It is 10:30. [time]
 b. It's September 1st. [date]
 c. It rains cats and dogs. [weather]
 d. It's really noisy in here. [situation]

Nonreferential *it* appears in cleft constructions.

Cleft

(2) **It was** Mary **who** finished off the leftovers.

Clausal Complement

Nonreferential *it* may offer an opinion about an event or a situation. Notice that nonreferential *it* refers to a clausal element: a gerund clause in (3a), an infinitive clause in (3b), or a *that* clause in (3c).

(3) a. It can be tiresome visiting relatives.

b. It is not a good idea to ask the secretary for his phone number.

c. Presidential candidate Mitt Romney's high school behavior is under scrutiny after it was unearthed that he took part in bullying a classmate.

19.2 Nonreferential *There*

Expletive

Nonreferential *there* appears in the subject position. It is a type of **expletive** subjects. It is placed before the string of [___ *be* NP].

(4) a. Beyond the volatile politics, there is a still fragile economy.

b. Nicolas Sarkozy said that there were too many foreigners in France and vowed to cut immigration.

Existential *there*

Nonreferential *there* may show the existence of somebody or something. It has been called existential *there*.

(5) a. There exists censorship.

b. There is a splinter in my spring roll.

Contraction

In spoken English or informal written English, modals or copular Vs may be contracted with nonreferential *there*.

(6) a. There's some milk left. ['s = is]

b. There's been a problem contacting the server. ['s = has]

c. There're a few things to discuss. ['re = are]

d. There'll be easier ways of doing this. ['ll = will]

e. There'd be very little Christianity. ['d = would]

f. There'd be trouble ahead. ['d = could]

In expletive *there* constructions, the V agrees with the head of its associated NP.

Agreement

(7) a. There is explicit formalism.

b. There lives a fisherman near the sea.

c. There are indications before experiencing nervous breakdown.

d. There begins some doubt in my mind as to whether he understood syntax.

e. There were a lot of people around here.

f. There are only a few left.

The following is an exception. There is a proximity effect in coordinated structures. The V agrees with the first conjunct.

Proximity

(8) a. There was [a fisherman and two lovely daughters] near the sea.

b. cf. [A fisherman and two lovely daughters] were near the sea.

(9) a. There were [two lovely daughters and a fisherman] near the sea.

b. cf. [Two lovely daughters and a fisherman] were near the sea.

There is may occur with some units of currency or time.

(10) a. There was twenty dollars and sixty cents in dimes.

b. There was still ten minutes before the train was due to start, and he thought he would walk up and down the platform.

New Information

Nonreferential *there* is used to introduce new information.

(11) There are, broadly speaking, two conceptual frameworks for how we approach child-rearing: The *village*, as popularized by Hillary Clinton's 1996 book on parenting, and the *family*, as conceived by cultural conservatives such as Rick Santorum.

Place Adverbial

In the following, *there* is a place adverbial.

(12) a. The meeting is at Bill's, and I promised to be there.

b. The books in his office were scattered here and there.

c. Robin was there as Aung San Suu Kyi arrived in Bangkok, taking her first foreign trip in 24 years.

Nonreferential *there* may appear with Vs such as {*appear, seem*, *run*}.

(13) a. There appear to be no family law decisions among the published opinions released today.

b. There seems to be great potential for two-way trade.

c. There ran down the street two joggers.

19.3 Focus Structures

Cleft

Clefting is a rule by which a canonical sentence as in (14a) is divided into two parts. The focused element is placed in the foreground position, and the other in the background position. The foreground position receives phonetic prominence. Cleft sentences have two basic types: *it* clefts as in (14b) and wh-clefts as in (14c).

(14) a. Police were investigating one of the string incidents on Monday as possible bias crimes.

b. **It was** [$_{\text{Foreground}}$ one of the string incidents] **that** [$_{\text{Background}}$ police were investigating on Monday as possible bias crimes].

c. **What** [$_{\text{Background}}$ police were investigating on Monday as possible bias crimes] **was** [$_{\text{Foreground}}$ one of the string incidents].

It cleft

What can be clefted in *it* clefts includes NPs as in (15a), place adverbials as in (15b), Advs as in (15c), *to* infinitive phrases as in (15d), and gerund clauses as in (15e).

(15) a. It was **Mary** who finished off the leftovers.

b. It was **at the market** that I saw Mary yesterday.

c. It was **greedily and speedily** that Fred drunk his beer.

d. It is **to address a far-reaching problem** that Ross is setting out to do.

e. It could be **going home early or slacking off work** that the boss reacted to.

Wh-cleft

What can be clefted in wh-clefts includes NPs as in (16a), infinitive complements as in (16b), interrogative complements as in (16c), gerund complements as in (16d), and VPs as in (16e).

(16) a. What Poirot could not help suspecting was a feeling of vigorously suppressed annoyance.

b. What he considered necessary was to cover all the furniture with cretonne, to put up curtains, to weed the garden, to make a little bridge on the pond, and to plant flowers.

c. What they completely failed to understand was why Zaphod was doing it.

d. What he could not stand was being pricked by the pins.

e. What he does is teach linguistics.

Reversed Wh-cleft

Many wh-clefts permit *reversed* wh-clefts. The focused element occurs at the beginning followed by [*be what*] as in (17a).

(17) a. [$_{\text{Foreground}}$ A valuable asset] is what I know.

b. What I know is [$_{\text{Foreground}}$ a valuable asset].

Fronting

Fronting is a movement rule by which an element is dislocated to the front of a sentence in order to make itself prominent. Some of the common elements which undergo fronting are object NPs as in (18a), PPs as in (18b), APs as in (18c), and complement clauses as in (18d) and (18e).

(18) a. All this information, Lucy digested.

b. Along the main line over the railway arch, a train thundered.

c. Successful, the efforts of the two women was.

d. That anything at all extraordinary could happen, it's hard to make her believe.

e. How he managed before Wladek arrived, Zaleski soon began to wonder.

Fronting is used to highlight a contrast.

(19) Baleful he looked, but happy he looked.

Inversion

Inversion is a movement rule by which the subject and an element change their position. There are three types: lexical inversion, stylistic inversion, and preposing-around-*be*.

Lexical

Lexical inversions are triggered by a particular word or phrase such as {*here, there, never, seldom, not only, nor, neither, so*} in formal contexts.

(20) a. And here comes the first of the clues I left you.

b. There goes the trumpet for the closing of the Gate.

c. Never have I tasted such a wonderful meal.

d. Seldom have we had such delight in strangers.

e. Not only was the weather fine—a really lovely summer's day—but I enjoyed the companionship of the man.

f. Nor can I remember, without laughing, the innocent admiration.

Stylistic

Stylistic inversions are alternatives to specific grammatical structures. For instance, (21a) is an alternative to the unreal conditional in (21b).

(21) a. Were I to fall in love, indeed, it would be a different thing, but I never have been in love.

b. If I were to fall in love, indeed, it would be a different thing, but I never have been in love.

Locative inversion in (22a) is a stylistic alternative to the canonical sentence in (22b).

(22) a. Down the hill rolled two joggers.

b. Two joggers rolled down the hill.

Preposing-around-*be*

Preposing-around-*be* is a type of inversion rules in order to comply with the End-Weight Principle.

(23) Dillon guessed that at issue were the ships under the Count de La Perouse, ships whose disappearance had shaken the entire world.

19.4 Coordination

Coordinator

In coordinated structures, there is a connector, called a **coordinator** such as {*and, or, but*}, in order to connect elements of the same type. As illustrated below, coordination may be phrasal as in (24a) or clausal as in (24b).

(24) a. The reality is that a body of religious and moral beliefs cannot [cohere **or** spread] without people to care for it.

b. [Neeleman could sometimes offend with his blunt words], **but** [his ideas were good enough to change the airline industry].

A single coordinator can connect more than two clauses.

(25) a. He cooked the lunch**,** he washed the dishes**, and** he looked after the children.

b. Get dressed**,** tidy up your room**, and** don't forget to make your bed.

Coordinators may be used in the sentence-initial position to start a new sentence and relate it to the previous sentence, against the prescriptive rule.

Descriptive Gr

(26) a. He must adapt and change it as he puts it into action. **And** finally, he must decide when to stop pushing the plan.

b. Neeleman believes ADD is one of the keys to his success. Far from regretting having it, he celebrates it. **But** he understands that he must manage his ADD carefully.

And establishes relationships of simple conjunction as in (27a), temporal ordering as in (27b), cause and effect as in (27c), condition as in (27d), concession as in (27e), and simultaneity as in (27f).

and

(27) a. He did some weeding **and** wrote a few pages of the paper.

b. I went to the store **and** bought some whiskey. [and then]

c. They eat that stuff **and** live to be a hundred. [and therefore]

d. You tell me what you've heard, **and** I'll tell you everything I've heard. [(if) ... then]

e. I can drink any amount of this **and** not get drunk. [and nevertheless]

f. Lucinda nibbled biscuits **and** read a book. [and at the same time]

or

Or is used for connecting possibilities or choices as in (28a). It is also used for saying what will happen if somebody does not do something as in (28b).

(28) a. He will eat them, **or** I will eat them. [alternatively]

b. Answer me, **or** I will reverse my judgment. [otherwise]

nor

Nor is used after a negative statement when adding another negative statement.

(29) She had **no** mind to be parted from him, **nor** for that matter had he any intention of being parted from her.

but, yet

{*But, Yet*} is a coordinator used for connecting two ideas or statements when the second one is different from the first one.

(30) a. Trying to keep prices low favors textile makers **but** is bad for farmers who grow the stuff.

b. Although, for her age, her health was good, **yet** she was old.

Some expressions can be connected by correlative conjunctions and other multiword conjunctions.

Correlative Conj

(31) a. **Both** the First Lady Michelle Obama **and** presidential candidate Mitt Romney delivered college commencement speeches on Saturday, but each speaker set a very different tone in addressing marriage equality.

b. He learns to accept that Anne's submission to Lady Russell was **neither** a symptom of weakness, **nor** cold-hearted prudence, but a further sign of principle and fortitude.

c. Perhaps the pills didn't work at first **and so** she took more of them.

d. A buzzy Time magazine story about Dr. Sears' parenting philosophy—**as well as** a fiery new polemic called "The Conflict: How Modern Motherhood Undermines the State of Women" by French philosopher Elisabeth Badinter—has stoked a fierce debate about whether cultural expectations of mothers have rolled back many of the social and political gains of the Second Wave feminist movement.

e. Your mind works **just as** mine does.

f. **Either** we fly over there **or** they fly over here. [alternative]

g. He aims at creating a new Britain—a Britain strong in its own power—ruled over, **not** by Germans, **but** by Englishmen. [contrast]

h. Especially in Europe, robust social welfare programs are designed **not only** to help parents care for their children, **but also** to help them maintain a fulfilling personal and professional life. [concession]

19.5 Conjunctive Adverbials

Conjunctive adverbials (= adverbial conjunctions) connect two clauses or sentences. They may appear at several positions in the sentence, separated from the rest by a comma or a set of commas. In this light, they are a type of adverbials.

(32) Government is often seen in America as a threat to family life.

a. That's not the case, **however**, in most other industrialized nations.

b. **However**, that's not the case in most other industrialized nations.

c. That's not the case in most other industrialized nations, **however**.

Conjunctive adverbials contribute to the cohesion of a discourse and express various types of relationships: ordering, summary, addition, exemplification, restatement, result, concession, contrast, attitude, and abrupt topic shift.

Ordering

Conjunctive adverbials of *ordering* signal the order of main points the speaker or writer wants to make.

(33) first, firstly, second, secondly, third, thirdly, next, then, finally

(34) Guidelines for Using Disposable Gloves: **First**, wash hands before putting on gloves or when changing to another pair. Gloves are not a substitute for proper hand washing. **Second**, remove and discard gloves, wash hands, and change to a clean pair of gloves after handling one food item and before starting work on another. In particular, never to fail to change gloves after handling raw meat, poultry, or seafood. Gloves are for single use only. Remember that the purpose of using gloves is to avoid cross-contamination. **Third**,

change to a clean pair of gloves whenever gloves become torn, soiled, or contaminated by contact with an unsanitary surface.

Conjunctive adverbials of *summary* signal a short account of something that gives only the most important information. Summary

(35) all in all, finally, in conclusion, in sum, in summary, overall, to conclude, to sum up, to summarize

(36) Daniels would, **in sum**, face an unusually acute version of a problem that has afflicted almost every other candidate in the Republican race.

Conjunctive adverbials of *addition* provide additional information to what has been said or written. Addition

(37) also, further, furthermore, in addition, moreover

(38) a. His affection for the region and its people is palpable. And **in addition**, he navigated many intricacies with the help of his erstwhile Iraqi government handler, whom Shadid decided to retain as a trusted employee after Saddam Hussein's fall.

b. Conversely, digital recordings do not degrade over time and, **furthermore**, add virtually no excess noise to the recordings.

Conjunctive adverbials of *exemplification* provide examples of something told or written before. Exemplification

(39) as an illustration, for example, for instance

(40) But from an industrial point of view—and exporters comprise a powerful lobby in Japan—the yen/won rate matters just as much.

Take the rivalries of Sony with Samsung or Honda with Hyundai, **for example**. From a Japanese standpoint, the South Koreans are far more cut-throat global competitors than American firms.

Restatement

Conjunctive adverbials of *restatement* are used to say or write something again in order to highlight it or make it clearer.

(41) in other words, namely, that is

(42) Such materials could also be used to protect hidden nuclear installations from the artificial equivalent of small earthquakes, **namely** bunker-busting bombs.

Result

Conjunctive adverbials of *result* provide information that is caused or produced due to the preceding information.

(43) accordingly, as a consequence, as a result, consequently, hence, so, therefore, thus

(44) The Committee expects moderate economic growth over coming quarters and **consequently** anticipates that the unemployment rate will decline gradually.

Concession

Conjunctive adverbials of *concession* provide information that you do not expect to obtain.

(45) despite that, in spite of that, nevertheless, nonetheless, still

(46) All of this appears to have given him a boost in the opinion polls. Caution is **nonetheless** in order.

Contrast

Conjunctive adverbials of *contrast* provide information that is very different in content, style or attitude with the previous information.

(47) by way of contrast, conversely, however, in contrast, instead

(48) Australian Shaun Wilson-Miller's film was originally intended to tell his friends he was dying, after his body rejected a second heart transplant, but a glitch uploaded the video to YouTube **instead**.

Attitude

Conjunctive adverbials of *attitude* describe the way that you think and feel about somebody or something.

(49) actually, as it happens, certainly, in actual fact, in fact, indeed

(50) Other tribes scorn the warlike Murle, who speak a distinct language and reputedly sided with the Arab north during Sudan's decades-long civil war. They are **certainly** fierce.

Abrupt Topic Shift

Conjunctive adverbials of *abrupt topic shift* denote a very sudden and unexpected conversion from one topic to another.

(51) apropos (of), by the by, by the way, incidentally

(52) This is what former Florida governor Jeb Bush was trying to tell his fellow Republicans when he observed, **apropos of** a recent discourse in the GOP primary: "It's a little troubling sometimes when people are appealing to people's fears and emotion rather than trying to get them to look over the horizon for a broader perspective, and that's kind of where we are."

19.6 Discourse Markers

Discourse markers are not an obligatory element of a sentence and are used in spoken English for a range of functions. Common discourse markers are *well, anyway, I mean, you know, oh, okay, right, like,* etc.

well

Well is used when continuing a conversation after a pause, or when you are pausing to consider your next words.

(53) His long-term plan for the Caps would be in tatters if they missed the playoffs, which seemed possible, and as for his basketball team, **well**, it is hard to know what to say about the Washington Wizards.

anyway

Anyway is used when adding something to support an idea or argument.

(54) I was feeling better then, but I wished I was out of there, **anyway**. I couldn't look up yet. **Well**, the woman fell to talking about how hard times was, and how poor they had to live.

I mean

I mean is used to clarify or correct what you have just said.

(55) What does she want with maps? **I mean**, what does she want them for?

you know

You know is used when you are giving extra information about something.

(56) She said, "Um, **you know**, I grew up with three brothers and that really toughens you up. And you don't complain."

You know is used while you think about what to say next.

(57) 'My God! What have I done? Dolly! For God's sake! ... You know ...' He could not go on; there was a sob in his throat.

oh

Oh is used when you pause because you are thinking about what you are going to say.

(58) When we finally reached Carlyle Brewing in the late afternoon, the bar was already crowded with beer aficionados. The beers on tap were tongue twisters: Humulus Lupulus IPA and Hophoria Double, for instance. We ordered a pint and settled into an adjacent room that was quiet and empty for about, oh, three minutes. A group of older men invaded.

Oh is used for accepting somebody's answer to your question.

(59) She knew little of the arts and graces of social life, which seemed to me to be a pity. "Would you like to come to the opera one night?" I asked. She smiled. "Would I understand it?" "Oh yes. I'll look and see what's on. I'll pick something light, and in English."

Oh is used for expressing an emotion such as surprise, anger, fear or happiness.

(60) 'She's still here,' she thought. 'What am I to say to her? Oh, dear! what have I done, what have I said? Why was I rude to her? What am I to do? What am I to say to her?' thought Kitty, and she stopped in the doorway.

okay — *Okay* is used when you want to start talking about something or want to continue it after a pause.

(61) "It's almost like going to a museum and standing in front of the masters and trying to do a copy of what work they've done, to really investigate what they did," he says. The language in translation casts its spell. After finishing *Hamlet* in Spanish, he turned to writing a new work of his own, in English. "For some reason, at the beginning, the characters were speaking to me in Spanish," he says. "**okay**, I need to write this in English, even though it's going to be translated into Spanish."

right — *Right* is used as a question tag for asking whether something you have said is correct.

(62) Now, Miss Eyelesbarrow, you went into the Long Barn to find some paint, **right**?

like — *Like* is used in very informal speech when you pause while you are thinking what to say next, explaining something, or giving an example of something.

(63) Besides, it never used to be right to mend clothes. Throw them away when they've got holes in them and buy new. The more stitches, the less riches. Isn't that right? Mending's anti-social. But it's all different here. It's like living, **like**, with lunatics. Everything they do is mad.

Exercise 19

19_1

Select the verb that best completes each sentence:

(64) There (is, are) a wide selection of art galleries in the town.

(65) There (is, are) even universities that offer courses in computer games as part of their curriculum.

(66) There (appear, appears) to be something wrong with the engine.

(67) There (seem, seems) to have been an accident.

19_2

Select the expression that best completes each sentence:

(68) The word (*nonetheless, and*) is a conjunctive adverb.

(69) All the following are subordinating conjunctions except *since, because, although*, (*when, nor*).

(70) All the following are conjunctive adverbs except *consequently, furthermore, therefore*, (*nevertheless, and*).

(71) The committee considered the letter, talked about its major points, and (the unanimous decision was made to ignore it, unanimously decided to ignore it).

19_3

Rewrite the sentences below, using expletive *it*:

(72) Eating too much is unhealthy.

(73) Looking after young children is tiring.

(74) Driving too fast is very dangerous.

19_4

Change each sentence into the corresponding *it* cleft sentence:

[e.g.] The Samsung Lions won the Korean Series in 2005.

[Answer: *It was the Samsung Lions that won the Korean Series in 2005*. OR *It was in 2005 that the Samsung Lions won the Korean Series*.]

(75) Negative political ads turned off a great many voters in the last election. [Cleft the subject.]

(76) Many country music stars have built their own theaters in Branson, Missouri. [Cleft the location.]

(77) Meeting Peter really started me off on this new line of work. [Cleft the subject.]

19_5

Change each sentence into the corresponding wh-cleft sentence:

[e.g.] This version of the story illustrates the author's originality.

[Answer: *What this version of the story illustrates is the author's originality*.]

(78) Human error caused the explosion.

(79) The poor condition of the lab equipment bothers me about chemistry class.

(80) You should ignore his sarcasm.

(81) The enormous influence of lobbyists turns some people against politics.

Conjunction Junction

[Words and Music by Bob Dorough]

Conjunction Junction, what's your function?
Hooking up words and phrases and clauses.
Conjunction Junction, how's that function?
I've got three favorite cars
That get most of my job done.
Conjunction Junction, what's their function?
I've got *and*, *but*, and *or*,
They'll get you pretty far.

And. That's an additive, like *this* and *that*.
But. That's sort of the opposite,
not *this* but *that*.
And then there's *or*
O-R, when you have a choice like
This or *that*
And, but, and *or*,
Get you pretty far.

Conjunction Junction, what's your function?
Hooking up two boxcars and making them run right.
Milk and honey, bread and butter, peas and rice,
Hey that's nice
Dirty but happy, digging and scratching,
Losing your shoe and a button or two
He's poor but honest, sad but true,
Boo-hoo-hoo-hoo-hoo!

20 Sentence Fragments, Fused Sentences, and Comma Splices

20.1 Sentence Fragments

Fragment

A fragment is a set of words that cannot stand alone as a complete independent sentence but starts with a capital letter and ends with a period. It is usually avoided in formal and written English.

In the following, as an answer to (1A), (1C) is recommended instead of (1B).

(1) A: Why are you so late?
    B: Because I overslept.
    C: It's because I overslept.

Ungrammatical

Fragments do not have a subject or V, or both. Below, the fragment does not express a complete thought.

(2) The Institute is well known as a conservative think-tank. Which had close ties to Presidents Reagan and Bush.

Revision

As shown in (3), the fragment in (2) can be corrected by replacing *it* for the subordinator to make an independent sentence or by linking the fragment to the preceding sentence.

(3) a. The Institute is well known as a conservative think-tank. It had close ties to Presidents Reagan and Bush.

b. The Institute is well known as a conservative think-tank, which had close ties to Presidents Reagan and Bush.

Deliberate Use

Because fragments are generally regarded errors in formal and written English, it is safer not to use them at all. But writers sometimes deliberately take advantage of fragments for literary emphasis. Fragments are also commonly used in advertisement.

(4) These are the kind of results you should expect from me. Because this is who I am.

(5) No connection? No outlet? Nowhere to sit? No problem. Introducing the TreoTM 650 smartphone by palmOne. It's the complete solution for wireless messaging, offering powerful email capabilities, text messaging, and a full-featured phone.

(6) We will take away his fleeting fame just as quickly as we gave it to him. No politics. No appeals. Just two superb fighters, trading punches once again before a howling crowd.

(7) "A woman has been strangled," she said. "In a train that has just passed. I saw it."

(8) "Do you know who you remind me of? Young Thomas Eade, our bank manager's son. Always out to shock people. It didn't do in banking circles, of course, so he went to the West Indies... He came home when his father died and inherited quite a lot of money. So nice for him. He was always better at spending money than making it."

You can revise fragments as complete sentences in at least two ways.

Tips

(9) a. Make the phrase into a sentence by adding the missing subject and/or V. This method elevates the importance of the fragment.

b. A fragment is almost always a continuation of the preceding sentence. Attach the fragment to the preceding sentence. This method establishes a relationship between the fragment and the sentence it is attached to.

Some examples of fragments are given below:

Ungrammatical

(10) a. We would have set to work that evening. Raising the ceiling, putting in a hardwood floor, and setting up the nets. [V-ingP]

b. When most strategists envision their businesses, they imagine a value chain. With inputs (costs) on the left and outputs (revenue) on the right. [PP]

c. In his new book, Fulsom recycles an outlandish rumor. The Nixon conspiracy with the mafia for killing JFK. [appositive]

d. The CEO had to take several steps to secure the facilities. And to protect employees. [compound predicate]

e. Researchers using MRI scans have found that people with ADD suffer a slightly diminished volume in four specific brain regions that have various functions. Such as modulating emotion and assisting in learning. [list]

Revision: Addition

You can add the missing subject and/or V, following the tip in (9a).

(11) a. We would have set to work that evening. We raised the ceiling, putting in a hardwood floor and setting up the nets.

b. When most strategists envision their businesses, they imagine a value chain. They imagine inputs (costs) on the left and outputs (revenue) on the right.

c. In his new book, Fulsom recycles an outlandish rumor. He uses Nixon conspiracy with the mafia for killing JFK.

d. The CEO had to take several steps to secure the facilities. He also had to protect employees.

e. Researchers using MRI scans have found that people with ADD suffer a slightly diminished volume in four specific brain regions that have various functions. Some examples of those functions are modulating emotion and assisting in learning.

Revision: Attachment

You can link the fragment to the preceding sentence, following the tip in (9b).

(12) a. We would have set to work that evening, raising the ceiling, putting in a hardwood floor, and setting up the nets.

b. When most strategists envision their businesses, they imagine a value chain with inputs (costs) on the left and outputs (revenue) on the right.

c. In his new book, Fulsom recycles an outlandish rumor that Nixon conspired with the mafia to have JFK killed.

d. The CEO had to take several steps to secure the facilities and to protect employees.

e. Researchers using MRI scans have found that people with ADD suffer a slightly diminished volume in four specific brain regions that have various functions such as modulating emotion and assisting in learning.

Tips

You can revise mistakenly punctuated subordinate clauses as sentences in at least two ways.

(13) a. Attach the fragment to the preceding sentence.

b. Remove the subordinating conjunction and add the missing expressions.

Ungrammatical

The following shows ungrammatical examples.

(14) a. The smell was already filling the room, a rich hot smell. Which seemed like an emanation from his early childhood.

b. People could move into houses. Where the lights worked and where the furnaces blew hot air up through grates at the touch of a finger on a button.

Revision: Attachment

You can link the fragment to the preceding sentence, following the tip in (13a).

(15) a. The smell was already filling the room, a rich hot smell which seemed like an emanation from his early childhood.

b. People could move into houses where the lights worked and where the furnaces blew hot air up through grates at the touch of a finger on a button.

Revision: Removal and Addition

You can remove the subordinating conjunction and add expressions, following the tip in (13b).

(16) a. The smell was already filling the room, a rich hot smell. That smell seemed like an emanation from his early childhood.

b. People could move into houses. In those places, the lights worked and the furnaces blew hot air up through grates at the touch of a finger on a button.

20.2 Fused Sentences and Comma Splices

Fused Sentence vs. Comma Splice

A *fused sentence* or a *comma splice* contains two independent clauses that have been incorrectly joined together. When two independent clauses are joined without using punctuation or a conjunction, the error is called a fused sentence. When two independent clauses are joined with a comma, the error is called a comma splice. In either case, the writer confuses the reader by incorrectly indicating the split-up between complete thoughts.

Ungrammatical

A *fused sentence* (often called a *run-on sentence*) or a *comma splice* (sometimes called a *comma fault*) appears when you are writing compound or compound-complex sentences.

(17) He was advocating freedom of speech he was crying hysterically that the revolution had been betrayed. [fused]

(18) He was advocating freedom of speech, he was crying hysterically that the revolution had been betrayed. [comma splice]

Put a period after each clause.

Revision: Period

(19) He was advocating freedom of speech. He was crying hysterically that the revolution had been betrayed.

Put a semicolon between clauses.

Revision: Semicolon

(20) He was advocating freedom of speech; he was crying hysterically that the revolution had been betrayed.

A comma can be inserted before a conjunction such as *and, but, or, nor, for, so,* or *yet.*

(21) Lemons were sour, so they set your teeth on edge even to smell them.

(22) Tracie threw Willie an old rug to cover himself with, for he still looked terribly pale.

One clause can be subordinated to the other.

(23) Lemons were so sour that they set your teeth on edge even to smell them.

(24) Because he still looked terribly pale, Tracie threw Willie an old rug to cover himself with.

One clause can become an introducing phrase.

(25) Because of his terribly pale look, Tracie threw Willie an old rug to cover himself with.

Comma, Conjunction, Semicolon, Period

A comma is used to separate things in a list, or is used between two clauses in a sentence. In the second use, it highlights similarity in thoughts and grammatical structures between the two clauses. A coordinating conjunction is a word that is used to join other words, phrases, clauses, and sentences. It specifies what kind of connection exists.

(26) SU PRED, and SU PRED.

A semicolon is used to separate words in a list, or different parts of a sentence that can be understood separately. It highlights the difference between thoughts that are related and grammatically equal.

(27) SU PRED; SU PRED.

A period separates two grammatically equal but unrelated units of thought.

(28) SU PRED. SU PRED.

Colon

Colons are used after a complete sentence to introduce a list or an explanation.

(29) "If you are looking for a bumper sticker to sum up how President Obama has handled what we inherited, it's pretty simple: Osama bin Laden is dead and General Motors is alive." [Vice President Biden]

Usually, a colon following a verb is unnecessary. (30a) should be revised as (30b).

(30) a. She needs: peas, baking potatoes, and stuffing.

b. She needs peas, baking potatoes, and stuffing.

Comma

When the clauses are short, parallel in form, and unified in thought, a comma (instead of a semicolon or a period) can link independent clauses not joined by a coordinating conjunction.

(31) a. They came, they fought, they died.

b. He had meant it, he had not merely said it, he had wished it.

c. He was abusing Big Brother, he was denouncing the dictatorship of the Party, he was demanding the immediate conclusion of peace with Eurasia, he was advocating freedom of speech, and he was crying hysterically that the revolution had been betrayed.

Exercise 20

20_1

Select the expression that best completes each sentence:

(32) All dependent clauses are (complete sentences, subordinate clauses).

(33) (*Coordination, Subordination*) is connecting two unequal but related clauses with a subordinating conjunction to form a complex sentence.

(34) Fragments also happen when a phrase is (added to, cut off from) the sentence it describes.

(35) A run-on sentence is the same as a (fragment, comma splice).

(36) When dependent clauses are introduced by a subordinating conjunction that comes before the independent clauses, the clauses are usually separated by a (comma, colon).

(37) Use a (semicolon, colon) before part of a sentence that explains what has just been stated.

(38) Use a semicolon between closely related (dependent, independent) clauses when the coordinating conjunction has been left out.

20_2

Add a comma, colon, or semicolon where it is needed to correct each sentence:

(39) James Matthew Barrie created this tale in 1904 however few people know the story behind its origin.

(40) David died at the age of fourteen James then tried to become a replacement for his dead brother.

(41) David never had a chance to grow up therefore like Peter Pan, he remained a boy forever to the members of his family.

(42) Barrie enjoyed the company of children thus he became attached to the five sons of his friends Sylvia and Arthur Llewelyn Davies.

(43) Unfortunately, the boys' parents died subsequently Barrie became their legal guardian.

(44) Margaret had a special name for Barrie she called him "my friendly."

(45) The Day of the Dead has Christian elements however it is originated in Aztec culture.

(46) Lilly has three favorite holidays Halloween Dia de los Muertos and Thanksgiving.

(47) Everyone visits their ancestors on this day the people even decorate the graveyards.

(48) Vendors sell all of the local favorites candy roasted corn and sweet drinks.

(49) The Mexicans believe that honoring the dead is necessary therefore they make an effort to participate in this special day.

20_3

Underline every sentential modifier, and add a comma, colon, semicolon, or period where it is needed to correct each sentence:

[e.g.] The first act in my opinion was much too slow.

[Answer: *The first act,* in my opinion, *was much too slow.*]

(50) The storm unfortunately did a great deal of damage.

(51) Glacier National Park for example is absolutely beautiful.

20_4

Revise each of the following sentences in several different ways, making any necessary changes:

(52) Women no longer need to colonize the traditionally male professions they have already opened most of the doors to the desirable career paths.

(53) She didn't know what to say to his announcement, she was not at a complete loss for words, either.

(54) I called for a reservation all the tables were taken.

20_5

Rewrite the following fragments as complete sentences:

(55) Reineck has a theory. Connected to actions by the United States government in the years before World War II began.

(56) Earhart was then given the assumed identity of Irene Bolam. So that no one would know she had been working as an American spy.

(57) Much of Reineck's work based on the research of a man named Joe Gervais.

(58) In addition, Bolam was wearing a medallion. Resembling one awarded to Earhart by President Herbert Hoover many years earlier.

(59) Stating, however, that her body must never be fingerprinted.

20_6

Rewrite the following fused sentences or comma splices as complete sentences:

(60) Computers make it possible to transmit information rapidly from one place to another, it is no longer necessary for employees working on the same project to be in the same place.

(61) For many people, the most convenient place to work is at home this eliminates having to commute to a workplace.

(62) They don't have to begin work at a specific time, they don't have to work for a fixed number of hours. (Try using the conjunction *nor*.)

(63) The old saying "out of sight, out of mind" is often true working at home may not be the best career move.

(64) Employees in an office can temporarily forget about unfinished chores at home, such as paying bills or doing housework, telecommuters find it more difficult to separate their home and work lives.

(65) Working at home usually saves money there are some extra expenses.

(66) Most telecommuters set aside a separate room in their homes to use as an office, they may also have to purchase office equipment, like a fax machine or a high-quality printer.

Unpack Your Adjectives

[Words and Music by George Newall]

Got home from camping last spring
Saw people, places and things
We barely had arrived,
Friends asked us to describe
The people, places and every last thing.
So we unpacked our adjectives.

I unpacked "frustrating" first.
Reached in and found the word "worst."
Then I picked "soggy" and
Next I picked "foggy" and
Then I was ready to tell them my tale.
'Cause I'd unpacked my adjectives.

Adjectives are words you use to really describe things
Handy words to carry around.
Days are sunny or they're rainy
Boys are dumb or else they're brainy
Adjectives can show you which way.

Adjectives are often used to help us compare things
To say how thin how fat how short how tall.
Girls who are tall can get taller,
Boys who are small can get smaller,
Till one is the tallest
And one is the smallest of all.

Bibliography

Beason, Larry and Mark Lester. 2012. *A commonsense guide to grammar and usage* (6th edition). Boston: Bedford/St. Martin's.

Carter, Ronald and Michael McCarthy. 2006. *Cambridge grammar of English*. Cambridge: Cambridge University Press.

Celce-Murcia, Marianne and Diane Larsen-Freeman. 1999. *The grammar book: An ESL/EFL teacher's course* (2nd edition). Boston: Heinle & Heinle Publishers.

DeCarrico, Jeanette S. 2000. *The structure of English: Studies in form and function for language teaching*. Ann Arbor: The University of Michigan Press.

Eastwood, John. 2006. *Intermediate Oxford practice grammar*. Oxford: Oxford University Press.

Fillmore, Charles J. 1986. Pragmatically controlled zero anaphora. In *Proceedings of the Berkeley Linguistic Society* 12, 95-107.

Glenn, Cheryl, Robert Keith Miller, and Suzanne Strobeck Webb. 2004. *Hodges' Harbrace handbook* (15th edition). Fort Worth: Harcourt College Publishers.

Greenbaum, Sidney and Randolph Quirk. 1990. *A student's grammar of the English language*. London: Longman.

Huddleston, Rodney and Geoffrey K. Pullum. 2002. *The Cambridge grammar of the English language*. Cambridge: Cambridge University Press.

Huddleston, Rodney and Geoffrey K. Pullum. 2005. *A student's introduction to English grammar*. Cambridge: Cambridge University Press.

Leech, Geoffrey and Jan Svartvik. 2002. *A communicative grammar of English* (3rd edition). London: Longman.

Quirk, Randolph, Sidney Greenbaum, Geoffrey Leech, and Jan Svartvik. 1985. *A comprehensive grammar of the English language*. London: Longman.

Thornbury, Scott. 2004. *Natural grammar*. Oxford: Oxford University Press.

Webb, Suzanne Strobeck, Robert Keith Miller, and Winifred Bryan Horner. 2001. *Hodges' Harbrace handbook* (14th edition). Fort Worth: Harcourt College Publishers.

Willis, Dave. 2004. *Collins Cobuild intermediate English grammar*. Glasgow: HarperCollins Publishers.

Yule, George. 2006. *Advanced Oxford practice grammar*. Oxford: Oxford University Press.

Index

When **Grammar** Meets **Linguistics**

지은이 | Jeong-Seok Kim

초판 1쇄 인쇄 | 2012년 8월 22일
초판 2쇄 인쇄 | 2016년 6월 01일

펴낸곳 | 세진무역
주　소 | 136-034 서울시 성북구 동소문동 4가 278-2 백호빌딩 301호
전　화 | 02-922-2111
팩　스 | 02-922-2113
전자우편 | sejintrc@hanafos.com

가　격 | 23,000원
ISBN 978-89-956507-4-5 (93740)